#ZUPTAS MUST FALL

and other rants

#ZUPTAS MUST FALL

and other rants

FRED KHUMALO

PENGUIN BOOKS

Published by Penguin Books
an imprint of Penguin Random House South Africa (Pty) Ltd
Reg. No. 1953/000441/07
The Estuaries No. 4, Oxbow Crescent, Century Avenue, Century City, 7441
PO Box 1144, Cape Town, 8000, South Africa

www.penguinbooks.co.za

First published 2016

1 3 5 7 9 10 8 6 4 2

Publication © Penguin Random House 2016
Text © Fred Khumalo 2016

PUBLISHER: Marlene Fryer
MANAGING EDITOR: Robert Plummer
EDITOR: Genevieve Adams
PROOFREADER: Bronwen Maynier
COVER DESIGNER: Gretchen van der Byl
TEXT DESIGNER: Ryan Africa

Set in 11.5 pt on 16 pt Adobe Garamond

Printed and bound by CTP Printers,
Duminy Street, Parow, 7500, South Africa

ISBN 978 1 77609 107 2 (print)
ISBN 978 1 77609 108 9 (ePub)

Contents

#TrevorNoahAllTheWay

What's with these Americans saying our boy Trevor Noah purloined a gag from Dave Chappelle and passed it as his own?

Crazy-ass dudes across the Atlantic got short memories. Or it's convenient for them to wallow in the bosom of Sister Amnesia. Let's claw back to the past, my friends, where the truth lies buried.

Years ago, dude by the name of Richard of the House of Pryor came to Africa. Hung out with some of my father's friends out in Nigeria. I know cos my pops took his mother's broom and flew from Durban to Nigeria after his boy Emeka out in Lagos blew his horn. It's a huge kudu horn that makes a unique sound only my father and a select few can decode. The decoded message was: Come to Lagos *urgently*.

When an African says 'urgently' then you know there's some shit flyin', cos we are so laid back and easy-going here we make the common garden snail seem like the new Usain Bolt. Rest of the world operates on a clock that has twenty-four hours. Ours has thirty. African time. Anyways, it's only half a day's travel by witch-broom from my end of Africa over to Nigeria.

But why did Emeka invite my father in the first place? Emeka needed some strong weed from the south cos this American crazy-dude Richard Pryor was having withdrawal symptoms: sweating and vomiting and crying out, 'Cocaine, please, give me cocaine, please, you motherfuckers.'

No cocaine in Nigeria at that time. And Nigerian weed was wack – not good enough for Pryor's debilitating condition.

So my pops gets onto his mother's broom, risking life and limb. It so happens that it's harmattan season in West Africa. My brothers from another mother in Nigeria will tell you what harmattan is. It's some shit Obama wouldn't wish even on Putin. Some nasty, diabolical shit, this harmattan. Something you certainly don't want happening to you, especially while you are airborne, flying on your mother's witch-broom.

Anyway, my father finally lands on the plush Ikoyi island in Lagos, spluttering and vomiting dust and shit. His friends rush at him with a calabash of palm wine. Introduce him to the Pryor character. My dad opens his camel-skin bag, gets out the required medication. His boy Emeka gets the pipe going.

And after a few puffs from my pop's pipe, Pryor is up and about. Full of verve and spunk and good ol' American jingoism. You know Americans. The less they know about something, the louder they are about that something. All in a sudden, nigger behaves like he's running the joint. All in a sudden, nigger tells my pops and the Nigerian crew that he is in Africa on a 'fact-finding mission'. His ethnographic assignment, as he calls it, has the blessings of a blacks-only college in Mississippi or some other Southern backwater. The raison d'être of the undertaking is to capture and preserve the nuances and character-building intimations of African storytelling in general and African humour in particular, and/or African word-play, including proverbs and idiomatic expressions, with the view to preserving these for the future cultural enrichment and inspirational possibilities of future generations of the black world in the diaspora. Sounding pseudo-scholarly, our boy Richard Pryor who dropped out of junior primary. The drug already creating a buzz inside his head.

So my pops and his boys in Nigeria start jawing and jawing, handing over their stories to a Western embezzler. On a platter.

Dude is holding some black contraption with shiny buttons and dials and needles and shit. My pop and his crew later gather this box is called a tape recorder. What this recorder thing does, it steals my pop's voice and all the stories that he grew up on. Can't say that these were my father's stories, per se. No. In Africa no one owns a story. Can you own the air that we breathe? (Well, come to think of it, that's exactly what the Americans are trying to do. One day they'll get it all figured out: how to patent and monopolise the air we breathe. But seeing that they can't do this yet, they come over and dump their chemicals and shit in our rivers, in our oceans. Just to spite us. So we can't breathe easily anyway. And then they bring their pharmaceuticals to cure us. At a price.)

Pop wants to shit himself when he hears his voice on this tape-recorder machine-thingy. Long story short, Pryor takes these tales – told in Zulu and Yoruba and Igbo – and modifies them so they sound American. Wynton Marsalis did the same. Just listen to *Congo Square*. That's our shit! Leastways, brother Wynton admits up front that what he's doing in that recording is African. Did we sue him? Did we say he stole our shit? No. Cos where we come from no one owns music. No one owns stories. Leastways (that's an American word by the way), no one owns jokes. Imaginate: 'Okay, ladies and gentlemen, I want to tell this joke, but let me phone my friend for his permission to tell this joke cos it belongs to him!'

Knock me down with a feather already! You own a joke?

Anyways, it's only much later when I get my head around this English language that I begin to understand what really went down under the baobab tree that fateful day during harmattan season. That nutcase Pryor stole our shit, took it home, and became rich and famous on it. You must listen to his gag about two cheetahs. Briefest summary: two cheetahs are at a watering hole when they spot a gazelle. One cheetah makes it known to his mate that he wouldn't mind a snack. But Mr Cheetah soon realises that what he is doing is a show of bad manners. So he says, 'Though I wouldn't mind a snack, let that not disturb our friendly conversation right now, mate.' So his friend says, 'How are the kids and wife?'

'Better than good,' says Mr Cheetah. 'In fact, that's why I'm talking about a snack. Simba, that's my little son, just shed his milk teeth. He needs some meat, something to chew on.'

On and on the cheetahs talk. Then the gazelle spots them. Starts running. The cheetahs look at the fleeing antelope with interest. Shrug their shoulders. Continue talking. Being considerate, you know. Giving the poor gazelle a head start. When he is a half a mile off, that's when they take off...

We told that shit first! It's *our* shit. You don't have no cheetahs in America, apart from the cheetahs you cheated us out of. We told that shit in Zulu, back when we couldn't speak English. And clever Pryor – suffering from American Artist Burnout – came here and we gave the shit to him on a platter. Cos we didn't know a man could steal no stories. A story is a story because it is shared. If there's no one to share it with, then it is no story at all. Artistic onanism I call it.

Anyways, my pops was livid when I told him that Pryor had taken their stories and was making money out of 'em. First off, pops can't understand the whole concept of people paying money (or, to use the African equivalent, giving cattle to a guy) just so he can tell you stories. But my dad soon recovers. Tells me, he says: 'When that nigger came to Nigeria and I had to take my mother's witch-broom to fly over there? And we made him smoke good weed from our part of the world? That was no weed at all. That was beetle dung mixed with camel urine and left to dry in the sun over a week. My supplier had run out of good weed so we had to improvise.'

Imaginate! I laughed the whole harvesting season. When we had to go to the market to sell our produce, I had nothing to sell because I'd been laughing the whole time other niggers be harvesting their shit. Now I could see why Pryor was such a crazymotherfucker.

You don't mess with beetle dung and camel urine. Ask me. Been there, done that. Got my private parts pierced while I was high on beetle shit.

You remember how Richard Pryor tried to burn himself? Beetle dung. And camel pee. And karma. Bad combination.

Now fast-forward fifty years: Dave Chappelle becomes a protégé of one Richard Pryor. He starts telling some gags to his fellow Americans. And before you can say, 'Osama Bin Laden, please meet George Bush,' the ignorant/myopic/amnesiac Americans think Chappelle is da bomb. Know what? All he did was dip into that collection that Pryor stole from Africa.

No coincidence that years later, when Chappelle got eclipsed by Kevin Hart and other dudes, he came to Africa. They said he'd come to these shores for a medical procedure. Medical procedure my black ass. Crazymotherfucker was hoping to pull a Richard Pryor on us. But we were wiser by this time. We set Boko Haram soldiers on the nigger's ass. Fled like Usain Bolt but didn't win no medal. When last did you hear of Dave Chappelle? A century ago. Now his peeps be tryna use our Trevor as a stepladder to put Dave Chappelle back on stage. Lame-ass attempt, motherfuckers. Know what? Get out of our business.

We can speaki Engilishi now. Can't fool us none. We got Boko Haram to harass your ass if you mess with our ass.

Other day I went down to my cave, got my DVD player (the one my Boko Haram brothers took from Dave Chappelle as he was fleeing – we use camel urine to power our electric generator). You won't believe this! Could recognise some of Chappelle's gags from the stories my pops used to tell us as we sat under a baobab tree, me and my boy Barry. Yeah, Barry now in the White House. Yes, *him*.

For a change, one American is telling the truth. Donald 'Is that a wig on your head?' Trump is right on the money when he says Barry was born in Africa. Barry be my boy from when we was this tall, when we was piccaninnies. Used to do things to camels, me and him. That's why Barry be so tall – years of trying to reach those camels.

Anyways, somebody suggested a long time ago that we should take Pryor to court for stealing our shit. But hell, we can't match Americans when it comes to juris ... juris-what? Think it's juris-credence. We can't match the Americans when it comes to matters of the law. People who sue their children for giving them hugs? Can't touch that! Yes, they sue McDonald's for making them obese. Can't touch that! They sue cigarette companies for giving them lung cancer. Can't touch that!

We can't even begin to sue them. We live in trees, right? Can't sue no one if you live in a tree and you consort with elephants and lions. Now that I mention it, when I encountered this lion the other day – mean-looking motherfucker – I considered taking him on as my lawyer. Bite those niggers and crackers across the Atlantic to bits. Or simply eat the evidence. Yeah, thought I, this lion would make a good lawyer. Until he opened his mouth. No teeth. Tooth-less lion. That a new one on me. Blame it on American-induced global warming. African lion been eatin' a lot of genetically modified American tourists, hence his teeth falling out.

Now, Trevor Noah tells our shit to those Americans like he remembers it, they say he stole it. Trevor speaks all eleven official South African languages. Twelve if you include Colouredese. Thirteen if you include Swahili. And how many languages do these Americans speak? Can't even speak English for shit.

'Get off of me!' Huh? Is that English? It's tomato sauce, not ketchup, you morons. It's plough, not plow. You 'fill in' forms, you don't 'fill out' forms. A trunk is the stuff at the bottom of a tree. The stuff at the back of your car is a boot. Yeah, a boot, not a trunk. Funny thing: these Americans call a woman's backside 'booty', yet they don't connect that with the back of a car. Duh!

I've worked too hard learning English, I can't have it dragged in the mud by the Americans. Let's protect the Queen's tongue as she is spake in the Empire! Well, former Empire. (Don't worry, Queen Lizzie, niggers in Africa have got your back. We're protecting the English language like you won't believe.)

Now, when my boy Trevor says something about being a connoisseur when it comes to spotting racism, they say he stole it from Dave Chappelle. Well, I got news for you: we got kicked in the ass by the racists long before there was something called America. We own copyright on pain and racism and shit. We're the original connoisseurs.

The turkey-eating dorks look intent on patenting every word in the dictionary. So you can't use the word 'race' and 'connoisseur' next to each other lest they accuse you of plagiarism. That's fucked up motherfuckers. Mind you, we don't speak like this in South Africa, so it's for the benefit of you dorks across the Atlantic. I can insult you in your language, but you can't insult me in my mother tongue. *Masend'amagusha! Mhlath'yezimpukane! Ndlebezembongolo!* (You sheep's testicles! You jaws of a fly! You donkey ears!)

Your Google Translate won't help you none. My language is light years ahead of your Stone Age Google. Yeah, my Zulu shit is too hot. Can't fucking touch this!

Hey, Mustafa, please load me another pipe of beetle dung. It's helping me remember a lot of things I'd thought were long buried under the sands of time.

I better start walking towards my cave. It's getting dark and I can hear those hyenas howling and approaching. Speaking of hyenas: the Americans even stole our hyenas and put them in that picture of theirs, *The Lion King*. And they talk to us about stealing stories. Nigger please! You don't even have hyenas in America. Hyenas! Hyenas are dime a dozen here in Africa. We don't want them no more. We're running out of food and they are stealing from our own mouths, the stinking rascals. Instead of asking us nicely for hyenas, the Americans invade our land in the night wearing night-vision goggles and take our hyenas. We wake up, our hyenas are in an American picture. Our hyenas and meerkats and Mufasa, too. Well, we didn't want Scar anyway. What do you do with an impotent male lion? Scar, they can take. Anytime. But to take Simba and Mufasa and our meerkats! It's like stealing the stripes from the American flag. And they talk to us about stealing stories.

It's a pity the United Nations headquarters are in America. The UN is part of the Illuminati, which protects and justifies American kleptocracy. The UN will never listen to us and how we've been stolen from, but they hyperventilate over Trevor allegedly pilfering from Chappelle. Nigger please.

Hey, Mustafa, don't behave like a forgetful American now. I said give me some beetle shit so I can smoke myself back to loquaciousness. I've run out of words.

Tweet this shit if you want, but just don't say you wrote it! The Americans have taught me well. Yeah, I went to Harvard. And you can google me. Just don't steal my stuff, tweet it all you want.

Sowetan, 24 October 2015

We've been having it!

While I was watching Trevor Noah's debut on *The Daily Show* on 28 September 2015, I was so happy to hear, when he spoke of his childhood in Soweto, that he and many of his neighbours had always shared a dream of having an indoor toilet.

Yes, whenever Joburg guys came down to Durban when I lived there as a kid and they would start playing big, we would have to remind them that they were not unlike many of our rural cousins who did their smelly business outside the house while those of us in KwaZulu-Natal townships (with the exception of KwaMashu and a few others) had toilets inside.

I was also ecstatic when Trevor pointed out that his Soweto had dusty streets. If you are my age and you grew up in Soweto, you might recall that even back then, well until the 1980s, many of the streets in that beguiling metropolis were unpaved. But in KwaZulu-Natal, a township without tarred roads and pavements looked odd. Durban's townships had tarred roads right from the outset.

And, of course, KwaZulu-Natal townships are famous for their love of trees. In Soweto, on the other hand, it's as if they were told it was a crime to plant a blade of grass, let alone a tree or a flower bed.

But anyway, when Noah said these things about toilets and dusty roads, I was reminded of that Vodacom advert with the pay-off line 'We've been having it'. Stupid regional jokes aside, we should be proud of the fact that, having taken the helm of *The Daily Show*, Noah has shown the world once again that South Africans have indeed 'been having it'. Give us a fair chance and we will demonstrate the true meaning of democracy. We're not approaching anyone with a begging bowl. We've got the talent, the chutzpah, sophistication and eye for business to get things done.

And in spite of decades of apartheid oppression and subjugation tainting our past, we've still been having it. You only have to look at Lucas 'Rhoo' Radebe, Anant Singh, Charlize Theron, Elon Musk and Mark Shuttleworth – to mention just a few of our people who have taken the world by storm since we emerged from our isolation.

But there are other heroes who made their mark overseas long before the collapse of apartheid: Steve 'Kalamazoo' Mokone, the legendary footballer and academic; Zakes Mokae, an unsung Hollywood hero if ever there was one; musicians Miriam Makeba, Hugh Masekela, Jonas Gwangwa, Letta Mbulu and Caiphus Semenya; and writer and intellectual Es'kia Mphahlele, who also inspired and guided the likes of Njabulo Ndebele, among others. We have certainly been having it.

But back to Noah. The country he has settled in has always proclaimed a multicultural identity, even though this is usually on its own terms. If you speak with an accent Americans don't 'get', or if you are Muslim or Chinese or Indian, they tend to raise their eyebrows at whatever you do. Yet wherever they go, they expect to be understood immediately. That's power for you. It breeds entitlement and arrogance.

So while you can go to the US to clean their toilets or sweep their streets, to take over an institution such as *The Daily Show* is considered by them to be the height of insolence, with the subtext of their disbelief generally being: 'Who's this nigger playing with the family jewels?'

The arts in general, and popular culture as represented by television and music in particular, are guarded jealously over there. When Hugh Masekela first visited the US and began playing jazz,

Miles Davis had to give him some advice on his style: 'Every time I saw him I told him to just keep on doing his own thing rather than trying to play what we were playing over here. After a while I think he started listening to me, because his playing got better.'[1] In retrospect, Masekela must be grateful that he heeded the Dark Prince's exhortation. After all, look where his African shit got him in America!

Americans are famously territorial, which is why I was nervous about Noah's reception, especially since the format of *The Daily Show* is fraught with danger for the host. Jon Stewart always used it to speak truth to power in a manner we have yet to see in South Africa through the medium of TV. I have said before that truth delivered on a platter of humour is a memorable dish, and Stewart did this with aplomb and alacrity. It also helped that he was white and American.

Noah, in contrast, offers a wholly different proposition. Not only is he black, but he is also from another country. And not only is he not American, he happens to be African, too. Those of us who have lived in the US are all too familiar with the prejudices that the people over there harbour towards Africans. My kids, who attended Cheery Middle School in Belmont, a suburb in the greater Boston area, were always asked by their classmates how come they spoke English so well and could use computers unaided – the implication being that computers cannot usually be operated from inside a cave. My daughter, who was fourteen at the time, played along with this perception of being from the bush, telling her friends that she missed her pet lion which she had left behind in Africa locked up in her cave. I kid you not when I tell you that the kids at her school actually lapped up the story and spread the word about how cool it was to hang out with their African friend who owned a lion as a pet.

Americans.

So if you're a foreigner in the US, especially an African, you have to prove that you are a thinking and progressive human being, and to do so as fast as you can – otherwise they immediately pigeon-hole you as someone who back home lived in a tree and consorted with giraffes. I am generalising of course. But underneath layers of generalisations tends to lie truth.

It becomes even more challenging when you're black and African in the US, since white Africans typically find it easier to insinuate themselves into American society. The general mindset, after all, favours whiteness. As Noah pointed out in his debut on *The Daily Show*, 'It feels like the family has a new stepdad ... and he's black, which is not ideal.'

That's why Americans will tolerate a white immigrant from Serbia with little education and no English at all, but they'll baulk at a professor from Africa who teaches English and philosophy at Harvard. This individual has to fight for the right to be heard. And it does not matter where this kind of prejudice occurs: it could be at a restaurant, an airport or a supermarket.

So let us congratulate Noah and give him all the support we can, because his success mirrors our determination as a people. It will hopefully also go a long way towards giving many other South Africans in different professional persuasions the chance to be heard out by societies and individuals who live beyond our own borders. With Noah now able to voice his opinions and demonstrate his talent on such a large international stage comes the opportunity for the rest of the world to finally learn what this country has to offer.

Sowetan, 2 October 2015

On a bus in America

Belmont, Massachusetts, USA

I had an authentic American experience on the bus home today. Stuff that you only see in movies. Spike Lee movies. Ed Griffin and David Chappelle stuff. Except this time it was for real – it wasn't scripted. It's the stuff you don't witness on a Harvard campus, where the denizens are so polite they apologise when you step on their shoes: 'Pardon me. Sorry that my foot was under your shoe.'

I was travelling from Watertown to Central Square, sitting just a few seats behind the driver for those who care for such details. It's the festive season and the bus was packed, but there was still space at the back. The problem was that there were people standing right up front, blocking the way for other passengers hoping to get a seat there, so the bus driver starts shouting, 'Move back please. Move back.'

And then the people behind me began yelling as well, in language as colourful as Christmas, like the guy immediately at my back: 'Motherfuckers blocking the way, this ain't yo mama's living room. Move the shit back!'

An elderly gentleman interjected, 'Please be patient. People are moving!' But someone in the fast-talking crowd behind me retorted, 'Who asked you, fucking cracker? Mind yo fuckin' business.'

The speaker of these flamboyant words was accompanied by four friends who began to yell their own comebacks at the old man. One was a woman carrying a baby in a pram who had earlier needed help to get it on board. ('*Shiit.* Can't a bitch get some help getting a baby on board a bus?') When someone finally assisted her, the grateful lady, aware of everyone else's eyes on her, shouted: 'What the fuck you lookin' at? You haven't seen a black bitch carrying a baby? Whatchu lookin' at?'

Like someone watching a fast game of tennis, my eyes moved from speaker to speaker as this group of pilgrims discussed, in voices posing a threat to the average ear drum, what they intended on doing once they got home. Their narrative, as an observant reader could surmise, was peppered with short words that began with 'f' or 's', as if those were the only ones that mattered in the dictionary, or in the entire lexicon of civilised humanity.

Eventually, when another gentleman outside of their circle suggested that perhaps, just perhaps, it would be preferable for them to eschew what he termed 'impolite speech', one of the pilgrims burst out, 'Now I can see why they lock black people up. I know exactly why. Black people be talkin' and mindin' their own business and some cracker be tellin' them, teachin' them how to talk. Cracker, I don't wanna be arrested so don't provoke me! Get the fuck out of my business!'

His female friend, aware of how dangerous the entire situation had become, jumped in with her own accusation: 'I know they be phoning the police right now, saying we being disorderly. No, we ain't done nothin' here. And I been recording this shit here on my iPhone. So no motherfucker be talkin' shit about us sayin' we started the shit. I ain't puttin' my ass in jail 'round Chrismas, no way!'

But an elderly man who had just climbed onto the bus had also been disturbed by this exchange of insalubrious words and decided to reprimand the speakers himself: 'Sir, there are young children here, if you don't mind your language.'

When one of the women heard this, she cried out triumphantly: 'Ah, this here cracker's got a Canadian accent! True, he got a accent. Speak up again, sir. What'd you say? I'm tellin' y'all he got a Canadian accent …'

To which her mate responded: 'What a Canadian accent gotta do with gettin' on the bus?'

Suddenly, the ice that had taken possession of the entire bus began to thaw and people started laughing. Shyly at first. Then in huge, bubbly gales.

When we got off at Central Square, I heard one of the brothers saying: 'Daaa'm these motherfuckers are fucking stuffy! I ain't visiting Cambridge again.' That's when it dawned on me that the pilgrims were not from the constipated confines of Harvard.

At the station I took the train to the university while they boarded the Downtown Boston train. It all made sense. But it had been so refreshing and authentic that for a minute I thought I was on a train to Manenberg in 'Kyaape Touuun'. Kyaape Toun, Manenberg!

Facebook, 20 December 2011

Ike Kekana Athlone, Mowbray, Kyaap…! Daar is n aap in die Kyaap!
Ntuthuko Khuzwayo Eish, I am trying to tranlate ngesiZulu. Mhh. Kunzima [It is difficult].
Colin Meyer Wow. That's the closest description of die kaap that i ever heard. The kaap has a word for these ppl – Ham. It is pronounced Gam and is to the kaap what nigga is to America. Brilliant. You made my day.
Zinhle Mugabe @Fred, was mimicking the American accent as I read this out loud. Thoroughly enjoyed it! How are you holding up with your Mzansi accent?
Phil Mhlongo I wonder what they say when they hear your accent, lol.
Ismail Mahomed Vivid pictures evoked by every word you write. I rode along on every word. What a superb journey from the soul of the US of A to the salt of the earthy Cape.

Waleed Ajouhaar Actually the real characters are on the taxis from Manenberg to Cape Town (bus passengers are a bit more civilized) just saying.

Heather Lewis @Ike Kekana – we are losing these Calls van die Kaap as more and more bureaucracy kills spontaneity and free spirits in the fruit and veggie and newspaper trade – I always liked: 'Mango, Mango, a woman can't go where a man go!' that they used to shout at The Stands at Claremont Station before they smartened the taxi ranks up. Someone should make a list, publish a little book so they aren't forgotten completely.

Yvonne Chengwe-Pupp Once got caught up in a scene similar to this one in a bus in Toronto. Jamaican ladies and some Canadian guys. Some serious action. Had to get involved when this rude Canadian guy started using the word Coon and monkeys to refer to black folks. One of those crazy streetcar rides.

John Diedrich Fred, beautiful. I am on a bus in Milwaukee right now and am encountering no such drama. Pity. You have the opening scene of a play here. Let's work out the rest of it New Year's Eve. See ya then. John.

Zulu psyche: an idiot's guide

At some stage in my career I wrote a column (see page 69) in which I warned the kwaito star Mshoza that she might rue the day she decided to bleach her skin à la Michael Jackson style. I had raised the topic out of concern for Mshoza's health, but many of my detractors pilloried me for my 'jealousy' – to the point that they insisted I apologise to her.

I'm not in the habit of apologising for an infraction I have not committed and I was not about to begin. For, let it be said here and now, I am from the kingdom by the sea. Over there, we choose our words carefully. Once chosen, we shall not withdraw those words.

However, this issue has left me with no choice but to revisit a theme I have touched upon in the past. I wish to introduce my readers to some isiZulu words that might, in due course, be part of our mainstream vocabulary as more and more people continue to embrace my mother tongue. These are words that you will hear on TV, or see on placards borne by hordes toyi-toying down a street near you. Knowledge of these terms will assist you in assessing the mood of the crowd you are dealing with if you are an official – or avoiding if you are a passer-by. For the purposes of this exercise I shall call this the 'A to Z idiot's guide to the Zulu psyche'. Our lesson begins below.

The 'A to Z idiot's guide to the Zulu psyche'

A is for *asikhokhi* – we are not paying! Everyone is talking about #FeesMustFall. How coy and apologetic. Are the fees going to fall by themselves? No. In my language we are direct: *asikhokhi.*

B is for *bhaxabula* – to beat a person vehemently, a favourite Zulu pastime. Synonyms for this word are *ukubhibiza, ukudukluza, ukubhonya.* We might just *bhaxabula* those who want us to pay.

C is for *(uku)cula* – singing. This is a national pastime since the man from Nkandla came to power. He sings his troubles away.

D is for *(isi)dudula* – a firm woman with a nice well-formed behind and good mounds on the chest area; a true African woman.

E is for *ehhe* – 'yes'. We like saying *ehhe,* especially when it is included in the sentence '*Ehhe, nokungebani nje kuloku kububula ngeNkandla, Nkandla.*' (Yes, everyone is murmuring about Nkandla, Nkandla.)

F is for *fihliza* – to demolish. Just what the EFF has promised to do to the ANC in the upcoming elections. We shall see.

G is for *(uku)gida* – traditional dancing, which has been the key preoccupation of the president since he came to power. Give that man a new pair of dancing shoes.

H is for *(e)hostela* – that's where you'll find many of my kinsmen: in the hostels. H is also for *(i)hlongandlebe* – the type of people we Zulus loathe. Stubborn, as if they were dropped on their heads when they were young. A typical *ihlongandlebe* is Julius Malema.

I is for *inyoka* – snake. Some members of the ANC apply this term to Malema. And we all know what to do to a snake – *fihliza* it. Which is what the ANC insists it will do to the EFF in the upcoming elections.

J is for *(i)jele* – jail. My people are afraid of jail, but our predilection for *ukubhaxabula* (see above) always lands us in *ejele*.

K is for *khuzeka* – 'please desist'. That's the plea we always make before we *bhaxabula* a person.

L is for *(i)landi* – one rand. We call it *ilandi* because there's no 'r' in our language.

M is for *(u)mantshingelane* – security guard. The word comes from a slight misunderstanding of the English phrase 'march in line', an instruction given to the first cohort of security guards recruited among my people. We make good *mantshingelanes*. Somebody tells me Mmusi Maimane is also a *mantshingelane* at that white building called the DA. Maybe it's a rumour spread by those who are 'eating jealous' for poor old Maimane. March in line, Maimane!

N is for *(uku)nqoba* – to be victorious. We love being victorious, no matter what the contest.

O is *Ofezela* – the Scorpions. Zuma evaded their sting ... just! Then he decided to shut them down, replacing them with hawks whose eyes he had plucked out. Hehehehe!

P is for *(i)phixiphixi* – a hypocrite. The best example of *amaphixiphixi* would be the leaders of COPE. Remember COPE? They were the guys who broke away from the ANC, apparently to defend the Constitution, when in fact they were actually serving in a regime that undermined that Constitution by using state resources to settle political scores.

Q is for *(i)qaba* – a barbarian. That's what gets a lot of people beaten up. Just because we can't speak Engilishi like a Engilishman, they call us Zulus barbarians. And they emerge from the experience with broken teeth. Highly *bhibizaed* and *bhaxabulaed*.

R is for … no. As I said earlier, we have no 'r' in Zulu. Light said Fled.

S is for *(uku)shaya* – to beat up. *Ukushaya* is a milder form of visiting violence upon an adversary. Why is my language so replete with synonyms for violent behaviour? *Hhayi!*

T is for *(ama)tekisi* – taxis. We have a monopoly in this business as drivers, queue marshals, *izinkabi* (enforcers) and, of course, as owners.

U is for *ukudla* – food. We love our stomachs.

V is for *(uku)vova inkani* – to frustrate a person. We derive pleasure from frustrating people. Just what the man from Nkandla did to Thuli Madonsela.

W is for *(uku)wina* – we love winning, too, whether it's in a debate, a stick fight, a race between taxis or the Lotto.

X is for *(uku)xoxa* – to converse. Having conversations is a favourite pastime as our good president has ably demonstrated. Every time he is asked about the Nkandla millions he tells a story.

Y is for *yehheni!* – an exclamation of surprise, as in '*Yehheni-bo! Nansi ingulube inginonela.*' (Golly gosh, this pig is getting too fat for me!) Or, to put it another way: 'This person is being quarrelsome with me and I have no option but to *bhibiza* him.'

Z is for *(uku)zuma* – a verb that means to ambush, or to surprise. Need I say more?

So, now that you've been enlightened about Zulu ways, why not hug that Zulu who's been standing on your stoep begging for your attention?

We ain't that bad, are we?

Rand Daily Mail **Online, 22 January 2016**

Alone among the Zulus:
an Englishwoman's experience

In her seminal book, *Alone Among the Zulus*, published in 1855, Catherine Barter wrote:

> For my own part, though I can speak Zulu correctly, I would gladly see it die out in Natal, for men who have the cleverness to understand such gibberish as they often hear would easily learn English, and so be enabled to proceed further to enlightenment. There is at this moment among the civilised natives of Natal a great desire to obtain English teaching for their children, and I have seen several who could read well in the Bible.
>
> I have myself had pupils who could write an English dictation in words of two and three syllables with very few mistakes, and one of them writes a tolerable English letter, and is able to read what is written in answer. The (Norwegian) missionary was a very active man. During my stay he made an expedition into the woods to cut down timber for building. He was away three days; his wife and I spent our evenings together; but oh! the difficulty of making ourselves understood to each other. She spoke Norwegian and I answered in English as a rule; but when words and gesticulations failed we had recourse to Zulu, in which we were both at home. Strange that a barbarous African dialect should form the only available means of communication between two European women.[1]

Now, dear reader, do me a favour: with a straight face, read that again. I tried, but every time I did, I spilled tea all over my desk, I was laughing so hard! A more delicious irony I have yet to encounter.

Needless to say, isiZulu is today the most widely spoken language in southern Africa, followed by isiXhosa and then Afrikaans; while English is only at number four. The biggest radio station in the country is Ukhozi, which broadcasts its programmes in isiZulu. And the biggest daily paper is *The Daily Sun*, which is scribbled, no doubt, in a version of English our Queen Barter wouldn't have approved of. (The third-largest daily paper in the country is *Isolezwe*, also an isiZulu paper.)[2] This Zulu gibberish has stood the test of time, hasn't it, Queen Barter?

Facebook, 4 December 2015

An open letter from a goat

Dear Black People,

It can't be with any other emotion but profound humility that I am scribbling this missive to you. After all, we are approaching the festive season when we goats have to be on our best behaviour.

Everywhere I turn, I hear the sound of whetstones as men sharpen their assegais and knives. One with no sense of history would wonder what battle these people are preparing for. But I have lived long enough to know that the war that is about to commence is the annual Terror on Goats.

Respectable men and women, many of them with children of their own, are readying themselves to wreak devastation on scores of goats like myself – all in the name of Christmas and New Year's festivities. Isn't Christmas supposed to be a time to celebrate the arrival of the Prince of Peace, that bearded son of Mary? Why the violence, then?

I am writing this letter from my corner of the goat shed at McDonald's Animal Farm in Richmond, where I was born. The yard is a hive of activity as I write, with people moving up and down, inspecting us for size. Oh how I wish I could be one of those roaming goats. Those cousins of mine know what to do around this time of year: they run to the mountains and stay there until the festive-season madness is over.

But there's no such luck for those of us born on farms. A spark of glee radiates from the eye of the farmer as he moves around the enclosures, rubbing his hands in anticipation of the huge profits he will make from our suffering. He mutters to himself, 'Yes, well fed, very well fed.'

The customer concurs: 'The ancestors will be pleased if I can appease them with that billy goat over there, the one with the twisted horns.'

Ancestors my foot! Why do the ancestors need a goat in order to consider their descendant's request for luck with the Lotto, or with that tender he's been eyeing all these years? Why us goats in particular?

Let me tell you how I have been able to elude the black man's pot all these years. Every time the customers come – mainly during Easter and December time – I always make a spectacle of myself. When a potential buyer, accompanied by my owner, approaches, I simply collapse on the ground and start foaming at the mouth, twitching my legs.

The would-be customer, startled, then backs away as if he's seen a ghost and proclaims, 'This one has been bewitched. It will bring bad luck to my house.' I know all about black people and their obsession with witchcraft, so I beat them at their own game.

Sometimes when a customer touches me from behind, I freeze for a while. Then, in slow motion, I turn around and stare at him. Again, he will jump out of his skin. 'Why isn't this goat jumping and bleating?'

See? I know the ropes.

Now these other mamparas in our compound will bleat until the entire KwaZulu-Natal province echoes with their cry, jumping up and down in the process. Their antics leave the customer bounding about in paroxysms of glee: 'That's the one! We want a goat that makes noise! A lively goat!'

A lively goat – so you can kill him! It's about as logical as hiring a finance minister only to fire him three days later.

But that's what they believe in, these black people: the more noise the goat makes as it is being slaughtered, the higher the reward from the ancestors. In vain have I tried to teach my colleagues to play retarded so that they won't be bought, but they won't listen.

But it doesn't matter anymore, anyway. I am writing this missive because I think my time has come. Things are no longer that easy for me. My bag of tricks is as empty as that of Mr Nkandla.

What really hurts me is that this genocide seems to be directed at only the goats; the sheep are always spared the knife. Even Jesus thinks they are cute. Thanks for nothing, you sheep sell-outs!

I can even understand the case of a cow being bought and killed. Black people love the meat. With goats, however, they kill us, and once the meat is cooked, they wrinkle their noses: 'Goat meat smells bad!' they say. So it seems as if they only slaughter us in the belief that our cries and our blood are the gateway to good luck and riches.

The other day I heard Julius Malema waxing loquacious about the high standards of civilisation in the United Kingdom, where he's just returned from. I like that word: civilisation. Juju Boy, can't you share with the other darkies your insight into English civilisation? Tell them the slaughter of goats is so last year. Let them eat sushi.

In fact, how about a national protest? #NoGoatsMustFall or #GoatsMustRoamFreely.

Do I have your ear, Juju? Earlier on I tried to attract Mmusi Maimane's attention. He looked the other way, covered his nose with his hand and muttered something about some broken president in a broken country.

You must know you're in trouble when even a party with three members refuses to disguise you as a human being and smuggle you out of Animal Farm so you can swell their ranks in preparation for next year's local elections.

Sowetan, 18 December 2015

NoViolet Bulawayo is wrong!
We don't need new names!

The other day a pale friend of mine, having heard my ramblings about the importance of first names in African culture, wanted to know the meaning of my given name, Vusisizwe.

Swelling with pride, like a vetkoek made of self-raising flour, I explained to her that it means 'the one who will rebuild the nation'. How profound, she said. Yeah, very optimistic and ambitious, I agreed. Black parents have a weird sense of humour. Why on earth would you give your child such a deep name?

There are other names I can think of that are equally questionable. Why would black parents give their boy child the name Cijimpi – 'the one who prepares for war'? Why on earth do you call your girl child Nomacala – 'the one who is in trouble with the law'? What are your reasons for naming your child Mxolisi – 'the one who apologises'? And why, pray tell, would you call your child Stilemalasiyashunqasibhek'eMpendle – 'the train is chugging along on its way to Impendle'?

And so we moved on to the names of other important people: Gedleyihlekisa, Jacob Zuma's name, means 'the one who smiles or laughs in your face while he is causing you physical harm' – a backstabber, in other words. My friend gasped in recognition.

Rolihlahla, Nelson Mandela's African name, means 'the one who drags a tree branch, leaving a cloud of dust in his wake' – or, to put it more bluntly, a shit-stirrer. At this stage my friend was in paroxysms of laughter.

Sello, Julius Malema's Sepedi name, means 'the cry' or 'the wail'. It was around this point that my friend remarked that African names seem to be very prophetic. Any coincidence that Malema is always crying out for attention?

Then she wanted to know the meaning of Ndumiso – as in Ndumiso Ngcobo. So I said, 'It means "the one with a big head".' She responded with an almost orgasmic sound of surprise. Sitting as we were in a public place, I realised it would be imprudent of me to take a lady to a point of no return right there and then. So I patted her shoulder reassuringly and told her I was only joking. Simplifying it, I explained that Ndumiso means 'praise'. Mondli, as in Makhanya, can be defined as 'the provider' – and the lowly newspaperman certainly provides the nation with something to chew on every week.

I am not making these things up. In fact, I found myself gasping in recognition as I stumbled on.

Merlot works in mysterious ways in winter, and I allowed the good vine to guide me to fecund valleys of creativity. We moved on to the names that were creating headlines at the time, such as those belonging to the Mandelas who are feuding about where the former statesman will be buried. I explained that the name Mandla means 'power' or 'might'. Ndaba, referring to Mandela's other grandson, means 'story'. Makaziwe, the name of Mandela's eldest daughter, means 'the one who needs to be known' – the tjatjarag attention-seeker. Nomzamo, Winnie Mandela's first name, can be defined as 'the one who came after many attempts'. Well, we all know Winnie's story.

Sitting back, my pale friend, being the imaginative writer that she is, observed: 'Fred, so African names are a story on their own; they are a narrative. Not like Jane and John in European culture.'

With that comment, I found myself even more determined to impress her, hoping to get to a higher level of companionship. I began digging in my memory bank for funny African names. Matlakala, which is a strangely popular name in Sesotho, means 'rubbish'. Mfanafuthi is Zulu for 'yet another boy'. Lovemore is Zimbabwean for 'give more love'. Perseverance, a favourite name for girls in Zimbabwe, means … exactly that, because Zimbabweans have a sense of humour even when their children are born in the gravest of times.

I also noted that our coloured friends have funny names which don't really mean anything: Trevor (as in Noah), Gareth (as in the dagga lawyer), Tyrone, Talip, Gatiep. My friend grasped that I was losing track of my narrative so she opened another bottle of Merlot, to put me back on course, you see.

Fortified by the nectar of the gods, I made off for firmer ground and explained to her that Kgalema, the name of the deputy president at the time, is a verb meaning 'to guide'. My friend noted sombrely that the man in the seat of power was gifted by the gods with a real guide on his side – a guide he is refusing to make use of.

I shrugged my shoulders and moved on to the next name: Buyelekhaya Dalindyebo. Now we were smoking! Buyelekhaya means 'go back home'. Dalindyebo means 'create wealth'. I am very worried that the king of the abaThembu, having been dethroned as I am told, has no home to go back to. Even the DA does not want him. If you get rejected by the DA there is no hope in hell that you can create any wealth. I just hope that the king will smoke a peace pipe with the ANC and the Mandelas so he can rightfully go back home.

Sunday World, 14 July 2013

This article was first published in 2013. In 2015, King Dalindyebo was sentenced to an effective twelve years' imprisonment for assaulting and setting fire to the homes of some of his subjects, kidnapping the family of one of his subjects, and defeating the ends of justice – acts which were committed by him while he was dispensing his own justice in his traditional court. But these acts, quite understandable and justifiable in traditional law, were found to be criminal under our Constitution, the supreme law of the land. Aren't we a fascinating country?

Ethnic cleansing will follow unchecked xenophobia

Our collective inertia in the face of the human catastrophe that is engulfing this nation has worked to remind me of Pastor Martin Niemöller's now legendary words about the atrocities committed by Hitler and his Nazis: 'First they came for the socialists, and I did not speak out – because I was not a socialist. Then they came for the trade unionists, and I did not speak out – because I was not a trade unionist. Then they came for the Jews, and I did not speak out – because I was not a Jew. Then they came for me – and there was no one left to speak for me.'

When the new wave of xenophobic attacks took place in Soweto in April 2015 – new, because the first real wave dates back to 2008 – many looked the other way, dismissing it as 'something that will pass'.

It did not. Like all good viruses, it moved around restlessly throughout the country, looking for a place where it could gain traction. It finally settled on KwaZulu-Natal, using the area as a springboard from which to relaunch its old hatred and infect the whole nation.

And it would not stop there. A new strain of the virus reared its head at Emalahleni informal settlement near Nancefield Hostel in Soweto. It was here that Florence Mukwevho fell victim to the virus. Her crime? She is Venda-speaking. She told the media that her assailants had shouted at her, 'We do not want Venda, Shangaan, Sotho and Tswana people.'

Given the general indifference or acquiescence that this country displays whenever a new wave of xenophobic attacks takes place, it is not surprising that many of the foreigners who lived here were desperate to get away. Now that they are gone or keeping their heads down, the bigots had to find another group which, in their warped minds, represented a 'threat from the outside'.

In a neighbourhood in KwaZulu-Natal dominated by Zulu speakers, this threat came in the form of non-Ngunis, who, as the popular refrains would have it, 'steal our jobs' and 'hinder our access to economic resources' – claims that are unashamedly myopic and pathetic in their self-entitlement. It had me thinking of an uncomfortably embarrassing experience I had when I was the editor at the then recently launched *Sunday World* in 1998.

The incident, which until a short time ago I had believed to be safely buried in the catacombs of my heart, involved me, Mondli Makhanya (my deputy at the time) and Bongani Keswa (the newspaper's former general manager), as well as an eminent black academic who will remain anonymous.

Still excited at the waves we were making in local journalism, my colleagues and I soon learned that our back-patting sessions were premature. We had, in just the first few months of our tenure at the paper, already committed a mammoth sin, and we didn't even know it.

This fact came to light in a letter addressed to the editor from the aforementioned academic, who was outraged at the fact that our new newspaper was nothing but a venture for Zulus. Keswa, Makhanya and I each occupied the top positions at the paper, and we also happened to be Zulus. This was evidently a matter that needed to be investigated, fumed the letter writer, who was a Tswana speaker. Was it because of a lack of duly educated and talented journalists in Gauteng, the writer asked, that Zulus should have to come all the way from KwaZulu-Natal to run a newspaper based in Johannesburg?

This could not be the case, because he went on to mention the names of eminent Tswana-speaking journalists with whom I had worked at *City Press* and other publications. He signed off with a promise that he would be laying a formal complaint about the matter with Zwelakhe Sisulu, one of the founders of New Africa Investments Limited, the former co-owners of *Sunday World*.

In the hustle and bustle of producing a newspaper, I never checked whether Sisulu ever received a letter from the academic. But this does not mean that I was not disturbed by his complaint. Disturbed, because when I took up the job – having been inter-viewed by a multiracial panel that included Aggrey Klaaste, Mike Tissong and Brian Pottinger – and then engaged the services of Makhanya as my deputy editor, not once did the thought cross my mind to intentionally surround myself with Zulus.

I simply wanted to produce a good paper, to work with the crème de la crème of local journalism. That the complainant pilloried Keswa for being from KwaZulu-Natal was most hilarious, given that the man (bless his soul) spoke the most corrupt version of Zulu imaginable – as do most Soweto-born Zulus I know.

The common generalisation about tribal chauvinism is that it is the province of uneducated, unsophisticated rustic bumpkins. Far from the truth. The fact that the individual who took it upon him-self to petition for the rights of all Tswana people (without actually consulting them) holds a doctorate and is attached to a prominent academic institution should tell you otherwise. That he took the trouble to write a complaint to our publication indicates that he might have discussed the matter with like-minded and possibly equally educated people who thought he was articulate enough to be the spokesman of their 'tribe'.

What is exposed in these kinds of encounters – in which fellow South Africans are vilified and condemned merely for speaking a dif-ferent language or having a different culture from their compatriots

– is that the viruses of bigotry and discrimination can infiltrate the tiniest or most unremarkable sectors of a culture, race or country. Even those who believe themselves least likely to be at the receiving end of racism or xenophobia might find their fortunes reversed during a new societal phase or conflict. This should help us to remember that each time we keep quiet when foreigners are attacked in our country, we are only making the ground fertile for the possible germination of other chauvinistic tendencies – or helping to rekindle the fires that we thought we had long extinguished, such as tribalism and regionalism.

Sing, hum or chant Pastor Niemöller's words as your daily mantra. Perhaps by doing this, your mind will stay focused and your conscience equally alert during these challenging times.

Rand Daily Mail Online, 24 April 2015

A Shangaan walks into a bar

Whenever a waiter gives him a half-full glass of wine, a friend of mine always retorts: 'Man, fill this glass up. My nose won't drown in the wine. I am not a white man.'

I don't mind when he makes the remark to a black waiter, even in the presence of our white friends, or, indeed, in the presence of his wife, who is of Caucasian persuasion.

But I do get worried when he makes the remark in front of white strangers, who might mistake him for a humourless racist.

In a racially sensitive country such as South Africa, one does need to be careful about the kind of ethnic or racial jokes or remarks one makes. The case of a guy in Klerksdorp who allegedly killed another man in May 2005 for calling him a Shangaan is instructive in this regard.

Over the years, and because they are in the minority, Shangaans have been the butt of many bad jokes. It's been said that they are stupid and have no fashion sense because they wear green shirts which they pair with yellow trousers and red shoes. Which is, of course, a sad and painful generalisation when you consider that there are many South Africans of Shangaan extraction who are brilliant businessmen, academics and entertainers, including Jomo Sono, Chicco Twala, Irvin Khoza, and writer and academic Chabani Manganyi.

Yet even in the face of such evidence to the contrary, you still get people who refer to an inferior form of polony or sausage sold in the townships as 'Shangaan wors'. In South Africa, then, if a person calls you a Shangaan, especially if you are not one, it is considered the height of insolence.

Ethnic stereotypes are not just the preserve of black society in South Africa, either. English and Afrikaans people have a number of barbs that they enjoy using on one another. Rooinek, rock spider, limey and pommy are just a few I can think of.

In the case of black South Africa – with the possible exception of the black population in Johannesburg, which has always been a melting pot – different ethnic groups were generally prevented from becoming acquainted with one another's languages and cultures because of apartheid laws such as the Influx Control Act and the Bantustan government system. This kind of segregation formed a breeding ground in many cultures for the creation of a number of acerbic ethnic insults and stereotypes. Zulus, for example, were dismissed as warlike and stupid. And the assumption that Zulu is a language of aggression continues to persist.

A few weeks ago, during a session in the National Assembly, deputy speaker Lechesa Tsenoli, losing his patience with members of the EFF, resorted to speaking Zulu when he reprimanded them: '*Uyabona-ke manje seniyedelela!*' (You see now, you're being insolent!)

He may have thought he was driving the fear of God into the EFF, but he actually did the opposite. For more than five minutes the House came to a standstill as Tsenoli was asked to withdraw the word '*delela*'. And guess what: a few days later T-shirts with *Delela!* emblazoned on them were being sold on street corners in downtown Johannesburg. Meanwhile, the *Delela* video has gone viral.

Had Tsenoli tried to control the EFF using his mother tongue, Sesotho, I doubt there would have been such a furore in the House.

The Nkandla imbroglio has also not helped to quell such stereotypical ideas about Zulus. If anything, it has only encouraged the belief that Zulus are wilfully stubborn people. After all, despite facing mounting evidence to the contrary, the man in question still doesn't concede any wrongdoing on his part in the saga.

Then there are the Sotho people, who have been victims of these kinds of offensive stereotypes as well. At the height of apartheid, many of them were considered cowards who spied on their black brethren on behalf of the white bosses at the mines and factories. Tswanas, in the meantime, were stingy and mean-spirited (it is said that in ancient times they would drown themselves rather than give their enemies the pleasure of beating them up). Swazis, like Tswanas, couldn't fight to save their lives. All they could do was insult their enemies 'until they stank'.

Friday was known as 'Boesman's Christmas' because of the perception that coloured people always spent their money on delicacies and booze on Fridays, which was payday, and were dirt poor by Monday. When Zulu people want to tell you how pitifully inebriated you are, they say: *'udakwe njengeNdiya elingenabhizinisi'* – you're as drunk as an Indian who has no business. This, of course, is based on the observation that serious Indians who run businesses – mostly Muslims – do not drink.

It is a given in any society intent on stratifying people according to race that those at its bottom layers tend to be vicious with one another. But with the demise of apartheid we have finally begun to realise that ethnic stereotypes are exactly that: stereotypes, not at all backed up by fact. In South Africa, at last, we have discovered our shared humanity, thank God.

Jokes can be a measure of a people's sense of maturity and sophistication, and it is healthy to be able to laugh at yourself occasionally. If you can't do this then outsiders will laugh at you. And it is painful when you get laughed at by 'the other'.

That is why I hate it when certain Americans make jokes about our president, but I don't mind if the jokes come from Trevor Noah or David Kau. Msholozi is ours, dammit. We reserve the right to put a showerhead on his head.

Go and create your own Nkandla and make fun of it, you tjatjarag Americans.

Sowetan, 5 September 2015

#ZuptasMustFall

Where I come from, when a person stumbles upon some good fortune, we say of him or her: *unyelwe yinyoni esandleni* (a bird shat in her hand). It's those people who have good *izinyanga* and *izangoma* (medicine men and women) who always stumble upon good luck. Whose hands are always sticky with bird shit.

I have many trees at home, and when my wife and kids are away, I stand under the trees with my arms outstretched, palms facing heavenwards, eyes closed. The birds will sing, chirp, flit about the branches, but never do they have the generosity and good sense to deposit their shit onto my hands. Damn them.

Now, my good friend Vytjie Mentor is sitting on a sofa inside the Gupta mansion the other day. Out of nowhere, a bird shits on her hand. And it's not just an accidental drop of poo. It's a mound.

Instead of jumping in celebration at the fact that her hand has just been weighed down by dollops of bird shit, she contorts her face in sheer disgust and rushes to the bathroom to wash it. Can you frigging believe this contumelious nincompoop? Some people are just ungrateful. She gets offered, out of the blue, the position of minister of public enterprises and she turns up her nose at it with an uppity 'No, thank you.' What tjatjaragness is this? What cheek!

And Mentor is not the only South African politician to have spurned the blessings that come with a handful of bird shit. Another Clever Black had a truckload of the stuff deposited in his hand and he didn't even bother to rush home to report that his ancestors were smiling down on him. He is that man with the forgettable name. Ag, what is it again? I know it reminds me of Jonah Lomu, except the man in question obviously can't be Jonah Lomu. Had he taken the job of minister of finance that was offered to him by the Zuptas, I probably wouldn't be forgetting his name like this ... Ah, I think it's Mcebisi, or maybe Mncedisi Jonas. Mbhexeshi Jonas? I don't know. But I am sure it is one of them.

I see that some of you are laughing, anxiety and confusion clouding your faces. What is this all about, you ask? Who is Vytjie Mentor, and why was she offered a ministerial position by the Zuptas? Who, pray tell, are the Zuptas? How different are they from the Guptas we've been hearing about?

Relevant questions, all of these, if you are a newcomer. It would be hard for anyone to keep track of what is going on with the Zuptas with the amount of information being thrown about lately. And because we serious authors are nowadays pitted against so many instant sources of information – Twitter, Snapchat, Facebook, Mgobhozi, Shwashwi – we have no option but to hit the ground running when we get a piece of news.

So unfortunately, unlike Thomas Hardy of yore, we cannot open a narrative by paying tribute to nature's bounteousness, or dedicate two pages of narration to the size of the mole on the villain's nose.

No, we don't tell. We show. We are Modern Authors. We go where the action is, for the juice, so that we can grab the reader by the throat – and only let go when we have their undivided attention. Then we sit back and start introducing the characters, recapitulating previous episodes of our long-running tale. Just like what I am about to do now.

If you have been following my contributions to the narrative called 'State of the Zupta Nation', you might be acquainted with some of its characters. You will probably be familiar with a few of the plot twists, and there are many. However, in order to be of service to literature, I cannot leave the rest of my readers at the mercy of speculation. Assumption, as young people would have it, is the mother of all fuck-ups. So if you are a member of the old crowd that has been following my ongoing story, do bear with me. Go to the fridge, fortify yourself with some strong beverage – you will definitely need it – while I introduce the neophytes to all the characters in this political circus. Here goes …

The Gupta family is a dynasty of business owners who migrated from the Indian state of Uttar Pradesh to South Africa in 1993, just a year before South Africa had its first democratic, all-inclusive elections (yes, newcomers, before 1994 only white people were recognised as true citizens of the Republic of South Africa and only they were allowed to vote).

Scientists tell us that water flows because of gravity. Social scientists tell us that people flow because of symbols. In the build-up to the elections, figures such as Archbishop Desmond Tutu were engaged in semiotics, selling the new South Africa as a rainbow nation where individuals of all colours, creeds, etc. would be represented and considered equals. This was powerful symbolism.

The positive vibes that were emanating from this country were what made up the minds of the adventurous Gupta family. We will go to South Africa to claim our own pot of gold at the end of that rainbow, they thought. And soon enough, they had set up their company, Sahara Computers, almost the minute they arrived here.

But it must be emphasised that even though we were being sold the concept of South Africa as the rainbow nation, this nation was not floating somewhere in the stratosphere. We were rooted in African soil. And the Guptas understood this immediately. They began to do things the 'African way', a concept which is founded on one specific principle: get as close to those in power as possible.

The Guptas, represented by one of the brothers, Ajay, began implementing this plan during Thabo Mbeki's presidency, obtaining

41

a place in his inner circle. In 2009, a pan-African magazine named *The Thinker* was launched. The magazine's editor was Dr Essop Pahad, Mbeki's long-time friend, ANC comrade and erstwhile minister in the presidency. Dr Pahad's magazine was funded by the Gupta family.

Two years earlier, in 2007, the son of current president Jacob Zuma, Duduzane Zuma, was asked to join the board of Sahara Computers. In 2009, the company received a tender for a government-subsidised supply of laptops to 300 000 teachers. In June 2010, *The New Age*, a daily newspaper that openly declared its partisanship with the ANC, was launched – and funded by the Guptas. (A television channel owned by the Guptas, ANN7, or African News Network7, would follow in 2013.)

Later in 2010, the *Mail & Guardian* reported that Gloria Bongi Ngema, President Zuma's fiancée at the time (and now his wife), had landed a job working for the Gupta family.[1]

Now if you are standing, please sit down. If you are already sitting, reach out for that liquid restorative, for things are beginning to heat up.

Weeks before *The New Age* launched, Themba Maseko, head of the Government Communication and Information System, received numerous requests from the Guptas for a meeting. On the day he finally gave in and was on his way to the Gupta home in Saxonwold, he got a call from the highest office in the land. Yes, the president himself came on the line. After greeting Maseko, Zuma said to him, *'Kuna labafana bakwaGupta, badinga uncedo lwakho. Ngicela ubancede.'* (There are these Gupta brothers who need your help. Please help them.)

'I was so pissed off and a bit unsettled,' Maseko told the *Sunday Times* in March 2016, reflecting on the conversation.

Maseko met Ajay Gupta and one of his brothers, whose name he could not recall during the interview. 'After niceties, Ajay said:

"We are setting up a newspaper called *The New Age*. I want government advertising channelled to the newspaper,"' Maseko says.

When Maseko baulked at the idea, citing procedure, Ajay Gupta would have none of it. 'Don't worry,' he said, 'tell us where the money is and tell departments to give you money and if they refuse we will deal with them. If you have a problem with any department, we will summon ministers here.'

Ordinarily, if a government functionary is confronted with a situation like this, he or she can simply run to the office of the president of the ruling party and report the miscreant. But what do you do if that president has just issued the instruction that you should help the miscreant?

A few weeks later, Maseko received a call from a senior staffer at *The New Age* who demanded a meeting with him. It was a Friday and Maseko was on his way to North West province for a family getaway. He told the newspaper employee to make an appointment with his office on Monday.

But the reporter responded, 'I'm not asking you. I am telling you. The meeting has to happen. It is urgent because of the launch of the TNA [*The New Age*].'

An hour later, Maseko would get a call from Ajay Gupta, who said to him, 'We are not asking you and actually, I want to meet you tomorrow [Saturday].'

When Maseko continued insisting that he could not make it to any meetings until the Monday after his golfing weekend, Ajay Gupta refused to accept his explanation. 'I am ordering you to meet tomorrow,' he told Maseko.

But Maseko, who had by now reached his boiling point, told Ajay Gupta to go and fuck himself. 'I told him that there were ANC leaders who owned media companies and they never behaved like that or gave me such instructions.'

Gupta's response was to threaten Maseko: 'I will talk to your seniors in government and you will be sorted out ... We will get you, we will replace you with people who will co-operate.'

A year later, Maseko was removed from his position as CEO of GCIS, where he had been in charge of a media-buying budget of just over R240 million a year.[2]

*

Your glass is empty. Replenish it, comrade. We are still in the second half of 2010, in October of that year, when ANC MP Vytjie Mentor got summoned to Johannesburg, ostensibly to meet with President Zuma in his capacity as the leader of her party.

On the day of her meeting, Mentor woke up at 3 a.m. to take a plane from Cape Town to Johannesburg. When she arrived, she was greeted at the airport by two men who were waiting for her with a board bearing her name. She got into the back of a black twin cab with them and started reading a newspaper. But before long, she realised that they were on the wrong route. They were not going to Luthuli House, the ANC headquarters in downtown Johannesburg, but were in the suburb of Saxonwold.

It was only then that she discovered that one of the gentlemen who had picked her up was a younger brother from the much-written-about Gupta family. This gentleman told her that President Zuma would be joining them, but that he was still held up at Luthuli House.

Speaking to the *Sunday Times* in 2016, Mentor recalled: 'I was then taken to meet a biggish guy who turned out to be Atul Gupta. We did not really know how to relate and made chit-chat. When I told him my son played cricket, he said they had a box at Newlands Cricket Ground.

'We then left the older brother behind and went to the home where a young Indian chef offered me food. By now I was agitated. It was almost 2pm. Then, the older brother [Atul Gupta] appeared.

By now I was very irritated. I told him it was not on. Was the president coming? If not, I wanted to go to the airport.'

When he heard this, Atul Gupta 'very quickly' told her what he wanted. He said that the South African Airways route to India was not very profitable and that the company needed a transformation. If Mentor got SAA to drop the route, he would make sure that she became a minister within a week.

'I was really, really, really, really shocked,' Mentor says, 'and turned him down. There are other details I'll reveal at the right time.'

Mentor says that it was only when she was leaving that the president came up to her, having entered the house from another entrance. She informed him immediately about what had transpired with the Guptas, though they tried to stop her as she did so – 'probably wanting to tell the president themselves,' she observes.

She continued with her story nonetheless. 'I told the president I could not do it; it was not correct ... We were talking amicably. There was no bad blood. I was angry with the Guptas, not with the president. He walked me down the stairs and to the car. I have not seen him since.'[3]

It is at this point, dear reader, that I have to remind you how we started this narrative. I may have laughed derisively at people who do not thank their gods when a bird shits in their hands, but I was being facetious, of course. This is serious stuff. If the proverbial bird delivers goodies which are suspect, I suggest you run for your life. Which is exactly what Mentor did.

*

So we move on. But before we do, let me remind you that this story, like all narratives worth their salt, has what we in the literary industry call 'flashbacks'. With your permission, I would like to flash back to 2013, in February of that year, when the Guptas threw a huge wedding in Johannesburg.

Ordinary South Africans going about their lives would not usually have been alerted to such an event – nor would they have cared about it – had it not been for the fact that the plane that had flown the Guptas' wedding guests from India to South Africa used Waterkloof Air Force Base in Pretoria as its landing base. The event raised eyebrows in many quarters, with newspaper front pages asking who exactly had authorised the landing when Waterkloof was a national key point and reserved for state guests.

Subsequent explanations indicated that the Guptas had initially applied for permission to land at O.R. Tambo International Airport, but this was not granted. They decided to get help from the august office of the Indian High Commission, which designated the Gupta wedding party an official delegation from their country. The private jet was then cleared to land at the Waterkloof military base 'based on false information and abuse of privileges', according to the findings of a panel of ministers tasked with investigating the incident, which has since become a major embarrassment for the South African government.[4]

When the president was taken to task about the affair, his spokespeople rallied around him, claiming that officials had wrongly used his name in the granting of permission for the landing.

Afterwards, Waterkloof seems to have receded into the background of popular news stories. South Africans, as we all know, are a very forgiving lot.

In 2014, however, another Gupta-related story broke, this time revealing that Eskom's deal to sponsor *The New Age*'s business breakfasts was deemed by auditors to be irregular. A few Eskom executives showed their unease about this, including Zola Tsotsi, who was chairman of Eskom at the time the controversial breakfasts were being sponsored. In March 2016, Tsotsi told an illuminating story about the Guptas' influence at the company: 'When I was proposed for reappointment for the second term, one of the Guptas simply called me and told me they will support my appointment and that without their support it will not happen. Two months after the appointment, they called me and said they will have me fired because I am not playing the game. I was forced to resign shortly after that.'

Tsotsi, according to the Guptas, was not playing ball. But what kind of ball was this? He explains further: 'They [the Guptas] wanted to supply gas through Eskom units in the Western Cape ... They wanted exclusivity. But others [businesses] had already signed memoranda of understanding with Eskom. I said to them I can't change that ... That's when they told me I don't support them.'5

I think you're beginning to understand, my dear visionary reader, why it is that the Guptas have been so powerful for so long. Why it is that they can hand out cabinet posts like matrons and madams handing out condoms at a brothel.

It is their mutually beneficial and symbiotic relationship with President Zuma himself that allows them to do this, and which prompted Godrich Gardee, an EFF MP, to stand up during the State of the Nation Address on 11 February 2016 and tell the president to sit down so he could raise a point of order.

'Sit down, Mr Zupta!' said Gardee, in the process christening a new campaign, the anti-Zupta bandwagon onto which many opponents of Zuma have since climbed.

Following Gardee's pronouncement, things went steadily downhill in Parliament that day as EFF supporters chanted together, 'Zupta must fall, Zupta must fall,' until they were led out of the House.

And if observers thought that what occurred on the EFF benches was just the usual madness for which this party of upstarts has come to be known, they were in for a surprise, for the ZuptasMustFall slogan had spawned an entire movement. All of a sudden, ZuptasMustFall graffiti was seen festooned on inner-city buildings in Cape Town and Johannesburg. Ever strategic and thinking on its feet (which is just another way of saying 'opportunistic'), the EFF rushed to the studio and recorded a song titled '#ZuptaMustFall', which went viral once it hit YouTube. In a statement following the release of the song, the EFF declared: 'Let everyone, everywhere, from all corners of our country join the clarion call that #Zupta-MustFall. From young people to old people, black and white, the unemployed, the poor, the urban and rural masses of our people let us speak and sing in one voice that #ZuptaMustFall.'[6]

Such was the impact of the entire ZuptasMustFall movement that the auditing firm KPMG, along with ABSA and FNB – the two banks with which the Guptas were associated – closed their accounts with Oakbay Investments, a Gupta company.

Dr Iraj Abedian, an economist, explained that the companies had probably been obliged to do this because of South African and international reporting laws, which require banks and auditors to not only sever relations with a company if they suspect illicit behaviour, but to report it as well.

If anything, it was surprising that it had taken so long for the companies to act, Abedian said.[7]

Finally, in a last-ditch effort to have the banks resume business with Oakbay, Duduzane Zuma stepped down as a shareholder and director of the company. This, Duduzane told the media in a statement released by Oakbay, was to help preserve the jobs of Oakbay's thousands of employees and to 'de-politicise' his participation in business. In his statement, Duduzane claims to have experienced the same history of hardship as other black South Africans. His career at Oakbay, he implies, was simply his attempt to be a productive member of his country.

I, like any other South African citizen, have constitutionally protected rights. My history and background is no different from that of all previously disadvantaged black people. The economy is necessarily skewed against us, which is the very basis of the struggle for political and economic emancipation. It is beyond dispute that our political miracle did not usher in an economic miracle for our people, hence the grinding poverty, unemployment and persisting inequality. Poverty in South Africa carries a black face and I didn't invent that. Notwithstanding my efforts to participate meaningfully in the economy, aspersions were cast on me and my family. As a result therefore, I have decided to relinquish all positions that I hold at Oakbay companies ... I will continue to be part of my generation whose mission is the economic emancipation of our people. This, my generation will achieve. Like our fathers achieved political liberation for us.

The statement goes on to emphasise how important Oakbay has been to the South African economy, having created over 3 500 jobs and employed more than 4 500 of the country's citizens. What is more, the Guptas affirmed, only a small portion of this success was down to their family's relationship with the government: 'The Gupta family has a 23-year history of strong business performance and turnaround skills. This strong performance has come almost entirely via successful activity in the private sector, with less than 1% of the Group's revenue coming from government contracts.'[8]

Lame PR intervention. I have successfully demonstrated how the Guptas' proximity to power has given them access to lucrative business from various government departments. They have used their connections with the president to their advantage – in a most brutal and unapologetic manner. One could argue that they have become the president's gatekeepers, deciding who he does business with and who gets appointed to what position. Their claims that they have landed their business deals on merit are ridiculous. They are playing with loaded dice.

*

So, comrades and friends, brothers and sisters, I am happy you have stayed with me for this long. I hope the exercise has been worth your while. Scribbling this narrative has certainly got my mind focused. It forced me to confront a few bare and brutal facts about our country's recent history, as well as to meditate on what it says about our future. In sitting down to tell this story, I was startled by how close those in power came to offering my country to the Guptas on a platter.

Thanks to the whistle-blowers and the media, it seems further damage has been prevented for now. At the time of writing, the Guptas were still busy doing damage control. A few members of the family had departed for the sandy shores of Dubai, probably to try to find a couple of banks that will do business with them.

Back at home in South Africa, the nation was chanting and dancing to the refrain of 'ZuptasMustFall, ZuptasMustFall, ZuptasMustFall'.

My king, oh my king

Whenever there is news about the Royal Family from that miserable thieving little island off the coast of Europe, I am reminded that I too have a king! King Goodwill Zwelithini kaBhekuzulu, 'the horned viper with the feathered head', who ascended the throne on 3 December 1971.

His reign has been mired in controversy since the beginning. In fact, during the period of his coronation, there was a concerted effort by the apartheid government to use him as a pawn to coerce tribal chiefs into becoming functionaries of the regime. At the same time, the royal house had to fight tooth and nail to remove him from the clutches of Mangosuthu Buthelezi who, they thought, was undermining the royal house by seeking to control the affairs of the young, naïve king.

As it happened, the king never got to finish his schooling, having been whisked away into hiding in the then KwaNdebele homeland in 1968 amid rumours that there was a plot to assassinate him. And so, as fate would have it, we ended up with an academically challenged king. But that's not what I'm writing about today.

When His Royal Highness Prince George Alexander Louis of Cambridge was introduced to the world as heir to the British throne, I suddenly realised, with much embarrassment, that I don't know who the heir to the Zulu throne is. In theory, the heir is the first son of the first wife (my king has six). Problem is, I couldn't remember the name of either the first wife or her first son.

A quick glance at *King of Goodwill: The Authorised Biography of King Goodwill Zwelithini kaBhekuzulu* reminded me that the first wife is Queen Sibongile Dlamini. I had to go to Wikipedia to be reminded that Queen Sibongile's son's name is Prince Lethukuthula.

Should I hang my head in shame for not knowing these basic facts about Zulu royalty? I think not. The Clever Black in me retorts: what have they done for me lately? However, the history-conscious South African of Zulu origin in me avers: in as far as I don't have any truck for royals of any nation, there's still something romantic about the institution. Perhaps it's the primordial yearning for something, or someone, to defer to.

As human beings we thrive on myths and symbols. Something that gives us that touchy-feely sensation that says 'we belong'; something the democratic institutions called governments cannot give us. Yes, our governments are there to ensure we have functioning countries; that those we elect to public office are accountable to the electorate. But over and above these establishments, the human heart yearns for some symbol.

The Brits have reduced this to a fine art. Royal worshipping is only rivalled in their country by religion, or football. Sometimes the three blend into one another seamlessly, so that the miserable little island is always in one fit of excitement or another. They need something, after all, to distract them from their terrible weather.

Unfortunately in South Africa, though many people speak proudly of their kings, our royal families – here I speak of everyone from the Tsongas to the Zulus, from the abaThembu to the ama-Ndebele, and everyone else in between – work very hard at making sure we can't respect them. A level-minded person simply can't defer to King Dalindyebo. I would daresay that even a traditional monarchist would find it difficult to revere a sixty-six-year-old man who impregnates an eighteen-year-old girl. King Zwelithini was that age when he married Queen Zola Zelusiwe Mafu. Mind you, the king's first son was born in 1970. That means he is fourteen years older than his 'mother', because in Zulu culture we don't speak of 'my father's other wife'; we simply say 'my other mother'.

In traditional Zulu culture I am not supposed to even contemplate such things, let alone make pronouncements on them. Thankfully, though, we live in a democracy. While we respect our kings, we hold the Constitution supreme. And the Constitution behoves us to speak out if the institutions that distinguish us as a nation – even ceremonial ones which include our royal families – are to make sense.

And the fact is, the royals in this country have denuded their institution of its respect and dignity. Maybe that's why we don't even bat an eyelid when the king marries his umpteenth wife. We can't be bothered no mo', as the Americans would say. Yes, we get angry when the king requests a couple of millions from the public purse to satisfy his flashy lifestyle, or when he goes to auctions and buys expensive buffaloes and oxen for his own kraal. Perhaps if he were working for us in some way or another, some of this anger could be ameliorated.

In case you are one of those Clever Blacks who wonder aloud why we have kings in this day and age, you should know that these institutions are protected in our Constitution, which was the work of a settlement based on compromise and agreed to by the ANC, the IFP, the NP and other minor parties at the historic pre-democracy talks. In the build-up to 1994, we made our bed, now we have to sleep in it. These royal institutions are not about to disappear.

The British royals take a lot of money from their taxpayers, but many of their subjects hold a begrudging respect towards them because they work hard at being their country's PR mascots, a pillar of unity and strength for the British people. You can insult David Cameron, the prime minister of the UK, all you want. But don't ever touch their royalty. It could be argued that the British royal family is the only symbolic unifier of the British people – be they liberals, conservatives or anarchists, they all genuflect at the feet of their royalty.

Maybe once our royals become useful we will remember their names and celebrate their birthdays. If I have spoken out of turn, it is because I want to regain respect for my king. *Wena weZulu! Bayede!*

Sunday World, **28 July 2013**

Walk tall, with Town Talk

A trip down memory lane. KwaZulu-Natal, circa 1978. Your mother had the neighbours salivating at the end of October the previous year when she had a brand new kitchen scheme from Ellerines and a dining-room suite from Town Talk delivered to your house.

Understandably, Christmas is splendiferous, neighbours and relatives from afar converging on the four-roomed castle of the Khumalos to oooh and aaah over the new acquisitions. Your mother is swelling with pride like a vetkoek made of self-raising flour as they praise her for her hard work. To further show them what she's made of, she bakes them the tastiest, most tear-jerkingly succulent scones on her new Glenwood coal stove, which she also bought from Town Talk two years ago. She's already paid it off, she doesn't omit to remind them. More ooohs and aaahs.

January comes and you and your siblings go back to school. February, you notice that your mother's tummy is big again. Damn these siblings. Why do they put themselves in your mom's stomach, knowing very well that at some stage they will have to come out! And when they do, what will the harvest be? Where do they think they are going to sleep? There are already four of you – six including your parents – in the two-bedroomed castle you call your home.

Anyway, by February your mother has stopped going to work. She must attend to the bloody growing tummy. The men from Town Talk and Ellerines arrive at your house on their scooters to collect money for the furniture. You've been seeing the trucks from these two stores descending on the neighbourhood since January to repossess furniture that was bought last November – right in time for Christmas. But this doesn't bother you because your mom pays the scooter men with a smile.

A month later, the scooter men come again. 'Where's your mother?' they ask you. You look in the bedroom because that's where she was a minute ago, but you can't find her. Dejected, the scooter man leaves the house. You're sitting in the kitchen enjoying sugared water with a slice of peanut-buttered bread when you hear a whisper: 'Is the man gone?' You look up: there's your mom, her head poking out of her bedroom door. She's a magician, is what you think about her.

Two weeks later, the scooter man is at the gate when your mom, who is standing in front of you and your two siblings, says: 'Tell the man I am not here.' Then she disappears into her bedroom. The man knocks, the door is opened. 'Children, where's your mom?' he demands. Before you, the eldest child, can answer, your tjatjarag little sister bursts out cheerfully, 'She said we must tell you she's not here.'

Can you relate to this boy's tale, non-white people?

Facebook, 5 March 2016

Luvuyo Nxokwana Fred, if I were Fred Khumalo I'd write a book that'll sell like hot cakes from primary and or high school level. These are stories of where South Africa comes from. Where their grandparents started before dining at McDonald's etc. These are stories that'll instil responsibilities in our next coming generation. I give this story 100% out of 100%. I had a full blown smile as I was reading and feeling fondly for our poor mothers. How they have raised us from nothing to something and most of them are not even there to taste their productions. Me, you and someone else. I suggest copyright this article. I see sales coming out flying. It is a friendly advice from a friend S'bhobhobho. I love it.

Tara Wells-Stoddard I do remember my mom flushing uncut diamonds down the toilet with the detective squad at the front door, circa 1978 Luipaardsvlei Mine, Krugersdorp.

Fred Khumalo Lovely, lovely.

Thami Ngidi The story of our lives Mntungwa. Yet we are here, still standing!

Mangi Magadla Watching a small black and white TV.

Fred Khumalo We come from afar, and people see us now and think we were born with silver spoons in our mouths!

Zakhele Gumede One of the Kunene brothers (you know him) had a similar kind of story. His main mission was to get the Ellerines brothers, who he was now meeting as colleagues in business, to bring back the furniture they took because it was overpriced and their HP terms were worse than modern day mashonisas [moneylenders/loan sharks].

Fred Khumalo Now, we're talking reparations!!!!

Renee Oelschig Of course. It is not a colour coded story. It happens to the very best of us!!!

Mohale Hullabaloo Majara Oh Fred, your story is so true to so many of us, every part of it. But that part about new siblings coming every second year made me laugh and cry all at the same time.

Siyabonga Hans Mthungwa, does she get the wet washing towel?

Fred Khumalo She gets a whistling swish from a peach tree. Shame, she was only six.

Zithulele Sibanyoni I can't relate to the Ellerines and Town Talk but what I do remember is a story involving a certain Gog' MaZondi. She was the village mashonisa. God help you if you couldn't pay ma Zondi on time. The whole of Pietermaritzburg would know your private parts, called private for a reason. She knew to describe them, in the most profane possible fashion, much to the horror of those within earshot. I swear, pun incidental, she would spare only the swear words not yet invented. And she spoke and looked like o' blom, the KZN version of the special branch. Cut a long story short, I concealed my mom's whereabouts a few times. It was my tjatjarag brother who gave the scheme away.

Doreen Gough I have white friends this has happened to – not the whole story, but definitely the repossession.

Zithulele Sibanyoni I do believe white people bought on hire purchase too. Otherwise how do you explain their love for vicious dogs? Methinks it was to scare the collections guy away. Sometimes having a vicious dog was killing two birds with one stone, if the collections guy was black.

Jennifer Cosslett This made me smile through tears. I love the writing and the story – it's beautiful but so flippingly heartbreakingly sad! At the same time, lessons like this build inner strength and resilience. Being moneyed isn't all it's cracked up to be. This I've learnt through teaching really really rich kids.

Zithulele Sibanyoni Being a repossessions guy must really have been a job for guys who were mad at the universe. How angry did you have to be to do THAT job? On second thoughts, former repossessions agents probably work for the Red Ants now.

Nolitha Peter One time my aunt gave the scooter guy 50 cents, then 2 seconds after he left, she gave me R2 to go to the shop – kwaMehlomane to buy things to cook for supper! I was sooo mad because the shop was really far for my skinny legs! She should have asked this man to give me a lift as he was going the same direction!!

Yoli Ndamase I just love your writings, Mntungwa.

Girl, you make
that dress look good

I was channel-surfing the other day when I stumbled upon what promised to be an interesting programme on BBC Entertainment.

What had grabbed my attention was the show's title: *Coupling*. Like a schoolboy about to raid the cookie jar, I felt highly excited, lowering the volume just in case my wife could hear the sounds that normally come with movies with such interesting titles as *Coupling*.

Having ascertained that Mrs K was in bed engaged in a telephone conversation, I felt relief coursing through me. I had the TV all to myself. But a few minutes into the programme, my heart sank. The coupling that I thought would take place on *Coupling* was not the kind of coupling that had set my heart racing in the first place.

Coupling was merely an innocent sitcom, but with that quintessentially English style of humour so dry you could grab a chunk of it, dunk it into your hot cup of coffee and only then enjoy it.

The story in a nutshell: in a moment of spontaneity, boy exchanges phone number with girl. After numerous conversations with himself, boy finally phones girl one night. We see her picking up the receiver and getting excited upon recognising his voice.

There is a long pause from his end. But it's not your 'I'm-gathering-my-thoughts' kind of pause. It's a 'can-someone-save-me-from-this-mess' pause. It's an 'oh-God-what's-wrong-with-me-why-did-I-phone-her' kind of pause.

He's one of those guys who want to get laid but possess a morbid fear of girls. There are many of those, trust me. It's a road I myself have travelled.

Meanwhile, the girl keeps prompting the boy calmly from the other end: 'I know you're there, keep talking.'

The vignette soon got me thinking about what I have previously written about men who are envious of President Jacob Zuma's bevy of women. Some men have admitted that, if they had their way – and the money, of course – they would also take more than one wife, just as our president has done.

I don't really know what happened during last weekend's reed dance when a group of girls apparently screamed and fainted upon seeing Zuma while attempting to throw themselves at him. And I don't want to trivialise the whole mysterious episode at all, but there are people who are suggesting that the president had overdosed on his *velabahleke* (the Zulu medicine that makes women weak at the knees) that morning, which is why those maidens screamed the way they did when he appeared. (On a more serious note, the episode does need a more thorough explanation. What happened there? Both the presidency and the royal house have been very quiet on the matter.)

But to move on, what I want to prove here, and as that TV programme so embarrassingly illustrates, is that women can drive the fear of God into the hearts of many men. If placed in a precarious position – in a social setting where they can't flash a beautiful car or buy an inappropriately expensive bottle of wine in order to make a statement – many men do not have the confidence and the requisite verbal skills to express themselves properly to women.

When I was younger, 'selling' yourself to a woman was a skill that was passed from generation to generation. This skill was and is still called *ukushela*.

For example, a popular saying Xhosa men use to sell themselves to women is '*Bli bli, mntanam uyagula, iyeza lakho ndim.*' (My girl, you are sick and I am your medicine.) The line turns them into commodities.

Zulu guys have a line for getting women, too, which is pretty trite by now: '*Umuhle engathi ugeza ngobisi, usule ngopholoni.*' (You are so beautiful, it's as if you bathe in milk and towel off with slices of polony.) I know, translated into English, this potent poetry sounds quite silly.

Other one-liners include: the path you are travelling is full of thorns so let me be your sandals. The sun is scorching and I'll be your umbrella. The sharks' teeth fall off when I approach the beach. Or what about: don't worry about the competitors – I am so tough, the crocodiles shit themselves when I plunge my foot into the river.

Duke Ellington, one of my favourite jazz composers, had some brilliant lines, too. One of them was: 'Girl, you make that dress look so beautiful.' Another declared: 'I didn't know angels could be so luscious.'[1]

A cousin of mine heard a guy his age throw this line at a passing woman: 'Yo, sweetiepie, Beyoncé tells me she wishes she were you. Don't you want me to be your Jay Z?'

It is clear that *ukushela*, like culture in general, keeps evolving. It can be also stressful when you don't know what to say. When you see a lady for the first time, you can't just exclaim to her: 'I love you!' Nor, God forbid, can you say: 'I like your hips, let's go to bed.'

Instead, you have to be charming, even if all you want is what I have just alluded to. Perhaps, gentlemen, we should stop stressing Number One about Nkandla and rather engage him on the cheerful subject of *ukushela*. How does he do it? Better yet, in this democratic, modern, non-sexist society, shouldn't women be the ones to make the first moves now? I know I speak for many when I say that men are tired of embarrassing themselves. Let women start doing the work.

Sowetan, 15 September 2015

Beyoncé: bringing cool to black pride

Although the children in the Khumalo family are encouraged to speak their minds, there are words that they know they can't use because they have the tendency to diminish the dignity of the speaker in the eyes of the listener.

That is why I had to do a double take when I heard my fifteen-year-old daughter mutter to herself, 'This shit is fucked up,' when I picked her up from school late last year.

Before I could say anything, she caught herself and apologised. I did not have to ask her what had tested her nerves, either. She was in such high dudgeon that the story came gushing out without any prompting on my part.

It turns out that one of the girls at her school had had a text conversation with her aunt in which she had written: 'I am getting tired of going to school with these black people.' The aunt responded with: 'They keep cropping all over like locusts. I thought Aids would have taken care of them.' To which her niece replied: 'Maybe ebola will.'

That's when I slammed on my brakes in utter shock. Was this true? How did my daughter find out about this chat, I wanted to know? She told me that the girl had erroneously shared the texts with other girls, one of whom happened to be black. The black girl, disappointed with her friend's racist drivel, took a screen grab of the conversation and posted it on Twitter. She also reported the matter to her parents, who took it up with the principal.

In a panic, the principal hastily organised a 'race sensitivity' workshop for the grade. Were the story to get out, it would be a PR disaster for this private Christian establishment.

However, the workshop lasted for only about thirty minutes, which is why my daughter was angry. On a previous occasion, when a few white students had been caught drunk, the school had conducted intensive workshops on alcohol abuse. When it was discovered that a few others had eating disorders, the school went to town organising workshops spread over three to four days.

'Now when it is about a really sensitive issue such as racism, which we live with every day, it's only thirty minutes. Every time there's a racist thing and we fight back, we get told we are overly sensitive, or being racist – when we are reacting to racism.'

These, my friends, are the words of a fifteen-year-old.

I am dredging up this incident in light of the controversy surrounding Beyoncé's music video for her new hit song 'Formation'. The release of the video has caused the white establishment in the States to accuse her of fomenting racial distrust in the country.

But all Beyoncé has done is highlight black resilience in the face of an uncaring white-dominated America. In her video, she uses old footage of black-owned houses being washed away by Hurricane Katrina, which razed large swathes of Louisiana, Mississippi and Alabama during the reign of King George W. of the Bush Dynasty in 2005. For shock value – this is entertainment after all – she sits on the roof of a cop car while it sinks into the water.

Mostly, though, she takes on stereotypes and slurs that get thrown at black people and embraces them – in this way, hurling them back at the abusers. She speaks of the food black people eat, the hairstyles that they wear and their 'Negro' noses 'with Jackson Five nostrils'.

What she is ultimately saying is: in the land of the brave and free, we still have to apologise for our poverty and wretchedness.

Why? In the land of liberty we have to apologise for being shot down by a belligerent racist police force. Why?

To get her point across, Beyoncé speaks in a language that white America might understand: the language of money. (Move over, Bill Gates, here's a black girl come to take your throne.) She tells her listeners to remain gracious and civil, reminding them that the best way to get back at those who judge them is with their 'paper' (black US slang for money).

To be honest, Beyoncé is not telling me anything I don't already know. In fact, I think she is being rather opportunistic. The political undertone of 'Formation' reminds me of her song 'Flawless', in which she samples novelist Chimamanda Ngozi Adichie's 'We Should All Be Feminists' speech. The song was a hit, thus becoming a fillip to Adichie's bestselling novel *Americanah*, and the cause of black feminism was put back into the mainstream. A win-win situation, you might say. But others might interject with the claim that Beyoncé is capitalising on black anger to line her own pockets.

Well, of course, is the response. She is in the business of making music and money, after all. And if in the process she happens to contribute to the fight by being a vehicle for black popular sentiment, why should we begrudge her? Rather, we should explore and utilise every avenue that keeps the black cause on course. If it takes a Beyoncé to espouse my daughter's frustration with the status quo, I am all for Beyoncé.

I do not want my daughter to keep apologising for being black. She is not being done a favour for being alive, for going to a school that is still predominantly white in a predominantly black country. It's her right, and I'm also paying top dollar to keep her there.

I am therefore happy that Beyoncé is bringing cool back to social commentary, her beautiful legs bestriding the confluence of art and politics.

Sowetan, **19 February 2016**

Ingenuity, Nigerian style

If I didn't know anything about Nigerian ingenuity, I would have dismissed the story I am about to tell you as top-drawer bunkum.

A few years ago, a friend of mine – a former Umkhonto we Sizwe soldier who is now a sought-after political consultant – was stuck in one of those notorious Lagosian traffic jams.

Having been victim to this inconvenience in the past, he had planned his day accordingly. He was therefore not worried about missing a few of his appointments while he sat sweating like a pig in his car, what with it being the middle of summer in Lagos.

An hour after he had left the airport, the traffic jam had come to a complete standstill. He channel-surfed the car radio, moving from Nigerian high-life stations and switching to African hip-hop stations to keep the boredom at bay. He was steadfastly refusing to be irritable.

But two hours later, he had moved only about 300 metres. Switching off the radio, he started singing to himself, drumming his fingers on the steering wheel. He decided it was the hum of the aircon driving him crazy, so he switched it off and rolled down his window in an attempt to get some fresh air, such as it was.

That's when it happened. The unmistakable stench of human waste hit him like a sledgehammer on his face. Before he could roll up his window, a man poked his head into the window.

A trained soldier, my friend reflexively moved to shut it. But it was one of those manually operated windows, so he couldn't move fast enough. Before he could attempt to do anything else, the intruder bellowed at him: 'Give me your wallet, or you get this!' In Johannesburg, the mugger would have been pointing a gun at my friend. But this was Lagos. In his gloved hand, the man held a fistful of excrement which he was getting ready to plaster all over my friend's face.

Stunned, my friend reached for his wallet, handing it over to the marauder, who immediately disappeared into the maze of cars.

When my friend first told this story more than five years ago, most of us in the group laughed it off as the malodorous product of his fertile imagination. But three years ago, another friend of ours visited Lagos, where he was to be stationed until early this year. During his tenure in that populous city, he witnessed at least one mugging where the victim was told to part with his wallet or have excrement plastered on his face. Right there in the middle of the city.

Even though I have travelled to Nigeria and worked for a Nigerian company, I fortunately have not witnessed any of these pungent encounters. Further, I have avoided retelling this tale in polite company because, first and foremost, it sounds far-fetched; secondly, it's not something you want to regale your friends with at a dinner table.

But with what has been happening in Cape Town of late – so-called protestors throwing human waste at their political opponents, or dumping the smelly mounds on the doorstep of Zille's offices – I felt obliged and somewhat liberated to share this tale with who-ever cares to listen. And when I finally told this story to a group of friends who hadn't heard it before, one of them said, 'So, those buggers in Cape Town are not being original after all.'

Yeah, the tjatjarag copycats in *die visdorpie* had to wait for the Nigerians to come up with something so simple yet powerful. If they don't co-operate, give them shit.

But even though they lack originality, I must give it to my cousins in Cape Town: it takes someone with balls to take his or her own home toilet bucket, walk to the train station, board a train with singing and ululating comrades, and then go and dump excrement at a targeted office in town. Yes, a few days ago scores of people were actually arrested at a train station carrying night-soil buckets.

Argh! Give these people a Bells for their balls.

In response to this fiasco, the chief of police in Cape Town – these Kaapenars are creative! – has launched an anti-excrement unit, a sub-unit of the anti-refugee contingent, which is modelled on the apartheid-era *dompas* squad – the same unit that would do random searches for people who did not have their *dompasses*. Now members of the anti-excrement unit are on the lookout for people carrying suspicious-looking buckets.

'Excuse me, sir, is that bucket full of sour milk, or your brown deposits?'

Just to be safe, the uniforms worn by members of the unit are made of plastic and their faces are covered with those scary masks reminiscent of the Saddam Hussein era when American and other Western soldiers went to Iraq in search of chemical weapons.

Come to think of it, what we are dealing with in Cape Town is an instance of biological warfare at its most basic. And when you are in the middle of a biological war, you know what you have to do: you supply your populace with masks and you create bunkers. But how do you deal with people throwing buckets with squishy brown stuff?

I wonder what these guys talk about after one of their raids. Perhaps something like, 'Comrade Stinky, did you see how the contents of my bucket put Zille's shoes to shame!'

I know, I know, it's not a comforting thought that in a country beset with so many challenges we should still be analysing shit on top of it. But unfortunately there it is, right there on our doorstep.

We can't ignore the smelly guerrillas. To paraphrase the poet Arthur Nortje, some must storm the castles, others describe the happening.

Imagine having a criminal record alluding to the fact that you were arrested for throwing a bucketful of the brown stuff at a public building! Now, there's a smelly thought …

Sowetan, 7 July 2013

Virgin brains

With temperatures soaring at around forty degrees over the past few weeks my face has turned completely navy – so much so that I've had to stay indoors, not only to avoid the sun, but also to stop children in the street from mistaking me for an apparition from outer space.

Under ordinary circumstances I am generally pretty dark. But with this fierce sun relentlessly hammering at me day in and day out, I find myself standing in front of the mirror with a smile and my eyes bulged out wide, just to remind myself that I am a human being and not a blob of blackness.

Which got me thinking. Since time immemorial, people have been holding beauty contests in which women, thin to the point of being almost transparent, have paraded themselves and won crowns and beautiful prizes.

Then somebody decided: stuff it, this is enough! We are going to have a beauty contest with 'bigger-sized' women. I use the word 'bigger-sized' because in America you get sued for calling someone fat. Even if they are. So you have to use euphemisms such as big-boned, differently sized, etc.

Anyway, whoever came up with this idea hit a bullseye. It worked like a charm. Now big is cool. Even designers of clothing lines have acknowledged this. There are women's shops that cater only for 'plus-sized' women.

Apparently inspired by this story of the rise of the underdog, somebody in Zimbabwe decided to hold a contest that would search for a Mr Ugly.

Jeez, I thought I'd seen ugly people in my life, but Zimbabwe showed me that they've got real talent in that department. In fact, the contestants were so ugly that President Mugabe was eliminated in the first round. (Mugabe enters every contest in his own country. Remember he won the country's first lotto some years ago?)

But now all these stories which advocate for the tolerance of difference have conspired to plant an idea in my head. It's a simple idea. I want to host a contest, too: one for the Blackest South African.

Even I know I'll never win that one. There are some serious contenders out there. Long before the heat wave, Home Affairs minister Malusi Gigaba was miles ahead of me in the blackness stakes. Ah, that brother is black.

Some years ago, when he was still president of the ANC Youth League, I interviewed him at his office in Luthuli House. Having registered my name at reception, I was escorted to his office upstairs. After waiting for him for some time, I started looking around his office, but that did not stop me from becoming impatient at the man's non-appearance. Suddenly, however, I heard someone close to me clearing his throat and a voice saying, 'I am here, brother.' I whirled around but still could not see anyone. Then somebody turned on the lights.

However, I soon realised that no one had actually switched on any lights. All that had happened was that Gigaba had smiled – and his smile had brought a brightness into the room. Upon seeing him up close, I muttered to myself: 'Well, I thought I was black, but this one takes the cup.'

So you see, the brother is *blaaaack*. But what a winning smile, which is why I am not hopeful about winning against him. I would not be able to enter anyway since I am the founder of the contest, the brains behind the concept. I have to give others a chance – I am no Mugabe, after all. I do hope to rope in Gigaba as one of the judges, however.

This story of blackness takes me directly to the issue of whiteness. I am sorry to disappoint you, but I am not going to discuss the statement Penny Sparrow made on Facebook in which she compares black people to monkeys. I can only say that it mystifies me that my fellow darkies are so hot under the collar at a sparrow having a dig at monkeys. I mean, it takes a lesser animal to recognise the bigger animals, doh!

No, the whiteness I want to talk about here is of a different hue (ignore the deliberately mixed metaphor and read on, dammit).

I recently came across an article in the *Sowetan* which claimed that doctors had warned Mshoza, the kwaito singer, to stay indoors or risk melting away like plastic in the heat wave. Apparently the quacks have pumped so much bleach and plastic into her body that the minute she walks into the sun, it begins to sizzle like bacon on a hot skillet ... Ssssssss.

In my language we have a beautiful expression: *ohlaba eyakhe akalelwa* (he who slaughters his own beast is not stopped). In this context, what Mshoza does with her body, and using her own money, does not and should not concern me. It's her own *indaba*. I'm sure she is fully conscious of what she is doing to herself by undergoing this series of surgical procedures.

During her interview, she showed her awareness of this fact when she laughingly told the *Sowetan* reporter: 'It's basically what Michael Jackson did. Right now, I am on pills and injections. I spend the day in the house drinking lots of water. It's a serious thing, if I expose myself to the sun, it might condemn me. I don't want to risk that.'[1]

But why would she risk the procedure in the first place when she knows what happened to Wacko Jacko? Black people are complicated. We spent years fighting against white supremacy and subjugation, but all along we were going to great lengths scrubbing our faces with skin lighteners so we could look like our oppressors. I know the Clever Blacks who read this will say I do not understand psychology, that I do not realise how the oppressed can unconsciously mimic and internalise their oppressors and all that deep convoluted crap.

But does Mshoza know what it means? I don't know because I have never spoken to her, and am not likely to. Being this blob of blackness that I am, I think seeing my face will give her a heart attack. I can't have a white black woman dying on my account.

Speaking of death, I suggest that in her will Mshoza tell her executors that her brain be donated to an academic hospital after she passes. Unlike other parts of her anatomy, her brains are clearly still virgin territory – unused. They should make for an interesting study.

Sowetan, 15 January 2016

What I meant was ...

There's a new word in Hollywood. Damonsplaining. This very rich addition to our dictionaries can be defined in a number of ways.

Damonsplaining (v.) – when a white man who claims to be advocating for change and diversity in the film industry browbeats an experienced film producer, who happens to be a black woman, into seeing diversity from his perspective.

Because you see, the Damonsplainer (n.) possesses the wisdom to identify, firstly, the discomfort of a victim in any situation. And, secondly, is blessed with the wherewithal to protect said victim from whatever discomfort he, in his eternal wisdom, has been able to identify. Especially if he, the Damonsplainer, is complicit in conditions that give rise to such discomfort.

In other words, those people who take it upon themselves to Damonsplain are like those who tell you that the rain is falling, and then go on to emphasise that only they know how vicious the rainfall is, and how best you can protect yourself from such rainfall. Another show of Damonsplaining was when Miley Cyrus tried to tell Nicki Minaj how to talk about racism.

Needless to say, Matt Damon, after whom the phenomenon is named, is not its true originator. He has merely taken it to new heights.

Steve Biko first identified Damonsplainers back in the 1960s. He would later go on to write in a South African Students' Organisation newsletter in August 1970: 'True to their image, the white liberals always knew what was good for the blacks and told them so. The wonder of it all is that the black people have believed in them for so long.'[1]

Ah, now we have an even clearer picture of the Damonsplainer. It is the white liberal! Yes, the one who has never supported apartheid. Yes, the one who always smiles at you at the office. Yes, the one who says you must dump your Christian/Western name because it is a slave name. Yes, the one who knows all about your problems – including how to solve them.

Now, let's recap. The setting of the Damonsplainer's slipup was the US television show *Project Greenlight*, a reality series that gives one inexperienced filmmaker the opportunity to direct a $3-million feature film. In the first episode of the series, a director of the film is chosen from a pool of contestants by a panel of industry experts. It must be added that this panel is made up almost entirely of white men, and includes Damon and Ben Affleck as judges. The film that was picked for the 2015 series of *Project Greenlight* was *Not Another Pretty Woman*, a romantic comedy about a white man who ends up marrying a black prostitute after getting left at the altar.

During the selection process, Effie Brown, the sole black member of the panel, and also the only woman, differed with the other panellists' choice. She was concerned about how the film might treat the black prostitute character, Harmony, who is abused by her white pimp. As an experienced member of the film industry, Brown said she wanted to ensure that the character would not fall into predictable clichés and stereotypes.

For this reason, she suggested that the job be given to the team of Leo Kei Angelos, a Vietnamese man, and Kristen Brancaccio, a woman. She felt that their experience in dealing with such sensitive issues as race and gender would help them to do justice to the prostitute character and to treat her with compassion, thus making a better movie because of this aspect.

But Damon was quick to interrupt Brown when she voiced this thought. She tried – you've gotta watch this! – at least three times to finish her point about diversity in the story, but the Damon behemoth would not relent, at one point word-vomiting: 'When we're talking about diversity, you do it in the casting of the film, not in the casting of the show.' At the end of his rant, Brown could only respond with, 'Wow, OK.'

You have to watch the clip.

*

For anyone who takes an interest in the goings-on of Hollywood and the celebrities who populate it, it is a well-established fact that transformation and diversity in the film industry still face major challenges. And this applies both behind the camera and in front of it.

The likes of Spike Lee, John Singleton and Tyler Perry have fought long and hard to populate the sets of their movies with some black faces in order to tell their stories from a different perspective. But it's been a long and arduous struggle.

The battles fought more than sixty years ago by Hollywood greats such as Paul Robeson, Sidney Poitier and Harry Belafonte have borne some fruit. Over the years, a small number of black men and women have had the opportunity to play lead characters in a few major Hollywood productions: from potboilers such as *Kiss the Girls* with Morgan Freeman, to more serious fare, such as *Cry, the Beloved Country* with James Earl Jones. But there's still major resistance within the industry from movie executives to cast more black protagonists in their movies.

The fight becomes harder and more complicated when members of the Tinseltown elite such as Damon – who always project a demeanour of tolerance and understanding towards their under-represented peers – begin to dig in their heels when true transformation is called for. After all, that's the nature of liberals: they provide you with a sense of false comfort, but when the chips are down and real change is being called for, then it has to be done on their own terms and at their own pace.

Facebook, 20 September 2015

I Facebook, therefore I am

Why I am Facebooking right now? I am Facebooking simply because I can. Do I need to be Facebooking? I doubt it. This technology is making us needlessly active when we could be expending our intellectual energy (such as it is!) in possibly more productive ways.

Facebook, 13 December 2011

Nkosikhulule Xhawulengweni Nyembezi I'm beginning to develop withdrawal syndrome because there is no 3G connection where I am.
Linda Lindikhaya Mndayi Do share the options when you think of some, sleepless and its sonop in Suid Afrika, besides inhouse push ups, no school lunches to prepare, FB is the next best thing.
Fred Khumalo Linda Lindikhaya Mndayi And you wonder how we survived without these things before! Amazing. Remember the days of TV1, and a combined TV2&3. And at 11pm they would shut the services, sing national anthem (not the current one. I am talking about the Stem). And it brought tears to your eyes, not because you liked the national anthem. But simply because you realised that this was the end of entertainment and you didn't have anywhere to go, and had no one to turn to. And you sat there looking at the screen, hoping for some magic. And all you could see on the screen was the signal that was basically telling you: motherfucker, go to sleep! What a fucking useless friendless life you lead! If you can't sleep you know what to do with those hands! The armed struggle, that's what I am referring to.

Kea Sebate Matane Wow Fred, i can relate to that and as u put it, what is this facebooking?

Fred Khumalo TV1 was for white people. And TV2&3 for darkies (Nguni languages and Sotho languages). And by sitting up that late watching white people on TV you had already broken the law!!! Remember we had Group Areas Act, and white people were not supposed to be in black neighbourhoods and vice versa. So, logically, by having those white faces in your living room you had undermined the blerry statutes of the Republic. Hahahaha! How we tolerated that shit so long is an embarrassing mystery. If you are in my age group, stop telling these stories to your kids because the esteem they hold you in diminishes with each telling of these tales. So, dear parent, stop!

Nduku Buthelezi How old is Mashobane kanti? I was discovered around the 70s but these tales aren't vivid as they are to Fred! Good to retell if no kid nearby, I agree.

Linda Lindikhaya Mndayi Lol can't cover it, so many real life memories brought. How some things creep up on one and soon seem std. Lovely trip down memory lane Fred, armed struggle notwithstanding

Sipho Sam But Fred...if we don't tell these tales you will have black kids who would not have a clue where this country comes from....and why it is the way it is....there would be no relation between the now... and the past struggle....there would be no connection between the Mandelas and Sobukwes if we don't tell them such...about the segregated bus/train stops....about the mqombothi that had to be hidden on the ground.....(and you dare walk over that piece of Zink!)......I mean imagine....your kid asking you 'Baba...UMandela.... udeme ngani?'.... [Daddy, what is Mandela famous for?]

Fred Khumalo Shenge, mina abazali bami badlala umacashelana kwaze konakala ngama-1960s. ITV iqale ngo-1976. Kodwa lena yethu thina bantu iqale later than that. Even after isiqalile, not many bantus could afford to buy their own sets. So, abanye bethu bebekhokha uzuka ukuze babuke uDeliwe noSenzekile ngefasitele kwamakhelwane.

Sengikhuluma ngalabo bethu basemalokishini nasemijondolo. [Shenge (Buthelezi clan name), my parents started playing their hide-and-seek games, and I was conceived in the 1960s. TV got introduced to this country in 1976. But the programmes targeted at us blacks were introduced much later. Even after the introduction of these black programmes, not many black people had their own TV sets. As a result, some of us used to pay five cents so we could be allowed to watch *Deliwe* and *Senzekile* (two popular Zulu dramas of the time) through an open window at a neighbour's house. I am referring here to those of us who grew up in townships and shacklands.]

Fred Khumalo Sipho Sam you're of course right. I was just exaggerating a bit. Tell these stories to these cheeseboys so they know that the money that we are earning which they think grows on trees was fought for. In fact those imaginary trees that produce money were watered with the blood of many.

Kea Sebate Matane Being on Robben Island 2 days ago, can't help it but memories rekindled. Let's share with young minds in case they mistook us for supa moms/dads!

Sipho Sam Hahahaaaa....love the paying for watching TV part..... lmao!

Fred Khumalo @sipho sam again, when I tell my kids about watching TV through the window, from the neighbours' house, they raise their eyebrows in a manner that betrays disbelief. But when we go down to Durban and they speak to my parents, and my younger brothers and sisters, my brats say, 'Now, we believe you, dad. It's just that you have so many stories that sound incredible.' Life in the old country was incredible, and I haven't even told them a fraction of the stories!!!

Sipho Sam Remember that time you were dying to see....your 'Motsie'....think the series was called Mampodi....and you paid izuka yakho [your five cents]....only to find out at the climax of the story your neighbours' battery suddenly dies on all those watching....with no possibility of a refund...ai bekunzima [wow, was it tough].

Fred Khumalo Eish, Sipho now you remind me of the car battery that was used to charge the TV!!!! Yes, not many darkies had electricity at that time, so they used a car battery for their TV. And it would die as the TV 'story' is hurtling towards a climax.... No refund! You pay another five cents the following evening....

Fred Khumalo Sometimes the man of the house at the 'communal TV centre' would bring his friends around for a drink. On those occasions, the urchins from the neighbourhood would be shouted at and told to disappear. The man of the house would fail to acknowledge the fact that when days were dark he had accepted your five cent coins which went a long way towards securing him a quart of cold beer. Sheeit! Why am I remembering these things as if it were yesterday?

Njabulo Hlongwane Hey Guyz! Nikhipha umuntu esathi ucashile ngalezindaba. [Your stories are so hilarious, they can betray someone who is in hiding because they cannot help but to laugh out loud.] Those were the good old dayz!

Cindy Phillips Taylor I Facebook therefore I am ...

Fred Khumalo Cindy Taylor most profound, existentialist statement thus far...

Louise Prinsloo I'm hooked on FB!

Thulani Tshabalala At times when we watch Chiefs vs Pirates if the team supported by the man of de house was going down harshly we would be dismissed unceromoniously. Those were de days.

Heather Lewis I call it farcebook and you can't leave, even when you die.

Nopesika Hobb Uhmmm, true that.

David Muir Not true. ITV1 was for whiteys with no life, who loved programs about marine organisms. One began to wonder 'How many things about seals don't I already know?' I enjoy hearing from you. I am glad for all my FaceBook friends.

Fred Khumalo Bongi Bongz Welcome to the neighbourhood of madness and mayhem. I know every denizen in this hood, and I realise this is your first throat-clearing comment. Don't stop at clearing the throat, gal, tell us what's on your mind.

How Google made me
an intellectual eunuch

During my school years I was so popular I had people buying me lunch or offering to hook me up with a girl. When I started selling cigarettes in the school toilets, tough guys used to protect me from bullies who wanted to take my cigarettes without paying.

Even when I started working, my popularity showed no signs of flagging. It had dawned on me by this time that the people who I worked with did not actually love me the way I thought I was loved at school. Rather, they loved my head; they loved what I knew.

You see, I used to be a repository of information – some of it useful, some of it just fun-to-know stuff. And I couldn't curb my enthusiasm to show people how little they knew.

Bob Marley's mother's name? Cedella Booker. George Michael's real name? Georgios Kyriacos Panayiotou. The longest word in the English dictionary? Floccinaucinihilipilification is just one of them. It stands out because it is so sexy. It also means 'the action or habit of estimating something as worthless'.[1] To add to my list of talents, I could go one step further and spell these obscure words, baffling several speakers and readers of the English language.

Journalists are lazy researchers. So a colleague on deadline would shout from his desk: 'Khumalo, who was Verwoerd's traditional healer?'

After telling the lazy bugger that the man who gave Verwoerd medicine for political power was Khotso Sethuntsa, my colleague would merrily type away, assuring me, 'Khumalo, this whole week your drinks are on me.'

I helped people write smoking-hot love letters in exchange, of course, for a favour of one sort or another. At times, I would assist in writing business proposals.

When a person had to appear in court, I could brief them on the procedure. 'Don't sweat, brother, there are too many matters on the court roll. Your case won't be heard this week, even though they said you should be there. They're just exercising their power. While you're at it, I have a friend who can appear on your behalf *pro Deo*.'

People genuflected before me, stunned by my bottomless well of knowledge. When they thought I wasn't listening, they gushed about 'the very dark boy with a squeaky voice who had swallowed a dictionary and various volumes of *Encyclopaedia Britannica* when he was young. You must hear him talk about Sol Plaatje, John Dube, the Bambatha Rebellion, the sinking of the *Mendi* ...'

But then everything changed. Google came along.

Now ask any fool who the president of Kazakhstan is and at the click of a button they can tell you. The same applies if you need to know the capital of Belize. If you really want to be impressed, ask the search engine to recite the names of all the US presidents. It can do so in less time than it takes you to ask the question out loud.

You want to have a safe discreet abortion? Go to Google. You want a Russian wife without having to go to Russia? Google it. You want to make a bomb big and powerful enough to tear apart an ATM? Google has all the answers.

Then there's Google's doppelgänger, that tart named Siri. Oh my God, that grating voice of hers! I'm gonna shoot that bitch when I see her. She reminds me of myself when I was younger.

I am well aware that what seemed to be my apparently limitless knowledge, along with my tendency to proffer it at the slightest provocation, made a lot of people feel inadequate about themselves – especially those who had degrees when I was still in high school. But I personally never minded this.

So when that terrorist Timothy McVeigh killed all those people in Oklahoma in the US in 1995, I asked myself why he hadn't gone to the Google headquarters in California instead and razed everything to the ground, thereby preventing the company from becoming the intellectual powerhouse it is today. I would have been able to maintain my position of power and influence as a result. Now I'm just an intellectual eunuch.

But hey, there is some hope for me. Something has come along that has given me bucket loads of Schadenfreude. I can already feel my gonads growing back. Why? Because a study has just revealed the effects of this widespread reliability on Google on human intelligence. And while the search engine has gifted the ordinary person with access to countless amounts of knowledge, having all this knowledge has, ironically, also inflicted many people with something called digital amnesia.[2] In other words, Google has actually made people dumber. Viva to that!

The study, conducted on 6 000 people in six Western countries, looked at what these people did whenever they needed to remember a fact. Among the American test subjects, half said that they would try to look up the answer online before trying to remember it. And – wait for it! – 24 per cent said they would probably forget it again right afterwards.[3] Something that you acquire easily can abandon you just as easily.

Think about your friends. Do they even bother memorising your phone number? No. They save it on their phone. When they get a new one, they simply start this process all over again by asking their friends and (in some cases) lovers for the phone numbers still missing on their devices.

Try to give someone directions to your place. They'll ask you about coordinates and such rot. But they are in trouble if you can't remember the name of your street or, as is the case in many townships, your street doesn't have a name. You tell them, 'Turn right, pass a church, short left, short right, go round the circle, then pass a dog urinating but it's not your problem,' but it won't help them and they get lost anyway – because they have lost the ability to memorise instructions.

The dumb Google slaves. How good this study makes me feel about my intellectual prowess. I'm just not sure how to capitalise on it.

Maybe Google can provide me with an answer?

Sowetan, 30 October 2015

Sello Motloung I've never heard of most things you've mentioned above... especially Khotso Sethuntsa. His encounter with Verwoerd must be very interesting, if indeed he existed.

Fred Khumalo Hhawu, Sello Motloung, Khotso did exist. He had a house in Matatiele, he was Mosotho. He was so famous in the townships in the late 1970s that after June 16, he was the talk of the townships, my brother. Jacana Media Publishers have released a book on him. He is a fascinating character. Someone must write a play or a novel on his story – it needs that kind of dramatisation.

Sello Motloung I've just GOOGLED him. I will certainly get the book. To think that I was in Matatiele for a good three months, even visited its one room museum.

Carol Walljee Khotso Sethuntsa also had a large property close to Lusikisiki. There's a school and area named after him.

Fred Khumalo You GOOGLED HIM! Proves the thesis of this post: you trust faceless Google more than you trust your flesh and blood brother. All the more reason I must shoot Google when I see him.

Fred Khumalo Carol Walljee Witness! Thank you.

Sello Motloung So you're a wordsmith. Actually a wordkhumalo.

Carol Walljee Hmmmm lots of interesting information. There must be a psychological term for that. I suffer from it too. I remember the telephone number of the neighbours who lived next to my sister in Eldos in 1979. Totally useless information for me or anyone else.

Cedric Mabe Malume..you are a gem! Bra Ernest would possibly rave about you if you bought him a couple of ndukus. To put our opinion on the research about Google producing the laziest generation ever, the right thing to do is to press the 'like' button.

Thabo Mmamadimo Kgetja Mathiba But with all said I like the humour. You're my man Fred Khumalo.

Chris Drift Fred Khumalo, what's even worse to me is the fact that the same Google fundis can quickly look up something and once found they assume they know all. The lack of just plain general knowledge amongst people is worrisome and irritating. It has become very difficult to converse with peers as you always have to explain what you're talking about. Indeed I feel like you.

Cedric Mabe But then again, one needs to ask where does the fault lie. Is it in the lack of general knowledge quizzes that were once so popular in my time? Or could it be that at 13, my son's homework specifically says google and report that makes him so Google reliant? Or even worse, God forbid, the advent of economic progress has proved the adage 'no rich man has books in his house' true? Because somehow even the people I could engage when I was younger have grown dumber but richer. Doctors cannot comprehend the most basic of things one says in medicine. Ai, but we live on to observe, malume [uncle].

Nkululeko Moyo Ever knowing but learning nothing at all.

Tshire Kau Aiiiiiii, whenever I see something on your wall, I giggle before even reading it because I know there will be something 'then pass a dog that's urinating' hahahaaa.

Fred Khumalo Don't misunderstand me, Google is a good tool, to

86

double check something when you're in a hurry, or to kickstart your research into something. But it can't be the be all and end all. There are many inaccuracies that get posted online, and end up on Google, and people pick them up and regurgitate them over and over, mistaking them for the truth. So, Google can never be a crutch to end all crutches. Aneva, chomee, aneva!

Some gripes about technology

Somebody stop this technology train now, I want to get off! It feels like I am playing catch-up every day. Just when I find myself getting to grips with a new product, something else comes along that upstages the 'wonder' of the time. In fact, I resisted getting my nine-year-old daughter a BlackBerry for some time, not only because I thought it was expensive, but also because I believe it to be too showy.

What? Fred doesn't have a BlackBerry? No, I don't.

And now that I understand BlackBerry, my daughter is pressuring me to get her an iTouch. Why?

'I want to play music.'

'But you can do that on an iPod?'

'No, I also want to buy things online!'

'But you can do that on the laptop!'

'No, the laptop is cumbersome.'

'What are you going to be buying online, and where does all the money come from?'

'I have a dad, doh! He will put money into my account so I can buy stuff online!'

And so, comrades, it looks like I am losing this round. The whole house is ganging up against me. The other daughter (all twelve years of her) wants a Kindle Fire. Just six months ago she was all agog about the previous Kindle. Imagine if we'd bought it then. How long will this fervour for the Kindle Fire last before something new comes along? I always thought technological innovations were supposed to aid us in organising our lives. Having something like a BlackBerry should allow you to make calls, surf the net, write emails, play games, etc. But no, technological innovation has forced us to acquire as many gadgets as possible to carry out these tasks, instead of helping us to eliminate them so that we can centralise our activities in one instrument. I see colleagues with BlackBerrys, laptops, Kindle Fires and other thingamajigs, most of which I have thus far resisted the temptation to buy. My smartphone and laptop are more than enough to fulfil my everyday communication needs. But no, my friends tell me, 'You are behind!'

I read everything I can on new technology so that I can prove to them that I know a droid is not some new disease that manifests itself around your groin. However, none of this seems to be enough. You should see the pride one of my friends shows in his tablet. Doh, Moses – was it Moses? – or one of those biblical chaps with a big beard already wrote some famous novel or short story on a tablet made of stone. So look who's laughing now. Moses got there first, you technological freaks.

Facebook, 15 December 2011

Himmah Waxter Too late to stop the train, it's on auto pilot, brother.

Mzoxolo Myta Budaza Mnumzana uKhumalo, izibhalo zakho ziyakhumbuleka apha ekhaya, nyani-nyani! [Mister Khumalo, your writings are sorely missed here at home, truly, truly!]

Adele Cohen Branch Excellent description of how we always remain just behind technological advances! I agree though, that one should get what fulfils what you need to do. No more! Bad enough trying to process all the new information.

Makwane Ima Padi I think it's referred to as android and not droid .. But I could be wrong..overall you're spot on bra Fred.

Paddy Harper Mntungwa, technology is the best friend we geezers have.

Mpho Pulane Nakana Ja hey. It just never stops. I think its just enslaving us really, this technology. We've just become dependent on it and have unnecessary 'needs'.

Fred Khumalo Makwane Ima Padi you are a few weeks behind. It's now a droid, no longer android. Pick up any magazine on technology, and the advertisement will tell you about a droid. The tablet is a tab. You are a living manifestation of how gets left behind. Doh!

Fred Khumalo ...a living manifestation of how one gets left behind. I type faster than i can think???? illiteracy that comes with Facebook communication is creeping up on me.

Makwane Ima Padi Lol, I guess I just learnt americanese..tx!

VK VK Its duh not doh, ask the gals! lol!lol!lol!

Pat Ricky This is true and so hilarious Mntungwa...lol Gone r the days when a computer was seen as a gadget that can do almost everything. But nowadays it has to be supplemented by a smartphone, a laptop and not to forget the fancy tablet (which more or less do the same thing).

Fred Khumalo Vuyo Kuhlane I know everybody writes it as duh! But they are wrong! See, the dangers of herd mentality. It's actually 'doh!' Where does it come from? It comes from The Simpsons, that cartoon show. It was invented by Homer Simpson's character. I think in my previous life I was a teacher...I like attention to detail.

Mokgosi Makena Tablet ne! That thing is a handful.

Magda Kasyoka Wilson I say no no to BB torch and Kindle Fire for 12 year olds. I might be old fashioned like you. They should find that pleasure in simple things in life – e.g. reading books, telling/sharing stories, playing out in garden and being just kids.

Fred Khumalo Well, Magda Kasyoka Wilson, I've given in. Everyone at their school has BB and Kindle Fire, so my kids are feeling really out. Mind you, it's not as if the other kids are showing off or what, but it's the norm around here, so being new from South Africa we were shocked that these things are just like toys to children. That's the US for you.

Another dinosaur

It's shocking that a media personality of John Robbie's stature and experience is a denialist dinosaur who doubts the power of Twitter. Arab Spring! Steve Hofmeyr vs Chester Missing debacle! These and many other stories happened on Twitter first. Hallo, Johnnie Rip van Winkle, time to wake up now. I know, I miss my typewriter and telex too, but hey, my man, we gotta admit: we can't reverse things, can't shift the hands of time.

Don't let the over-forties side down, Johnnie Boy. Some of us conceded defeat a long time ago and embraced these technological innovations. In fact, a few of us are even better at using them than the kids who are supposedly running rings around us. So don't let the side down. If you have misgivings about Twitter, mention it among your friends, at home or at a pub – not on radio!

Facebook, 28 November 2014

Armstrong Ndlela Ask John Robbie to donate to a charitable fund of those that want to rebuild the Berlin Wall.

Fred Khumalo Looks like I'm pissing against the wind. John Robbie is not even on Facebook, by the look of things. So, this message won't reach him. Wake up, Johnnie Boy, wake up.

Glynis Mauldon Fred share this on the 702 Facebook page!!

Glynis Mauldon Better still, tweet Redi.....

Fred Khumalo Glynis Mauldon The deed is done! Redi Tlhabi

Glynis Mauldon I hate to confess Fred Khumalo I am not on Twitter... It must be an age thing ☺

Fred Khumalo Until about four, five years ago, a friend of mine who happens to be a radiographer, didn't know what an email was! And, wait for it, he is a member of the Gauteng legislature. I had to gently take him through the ropes! Glynis Mauldon

Glynis Mauldon Sure your friend is way younger than me Fred!!

Dumisani Muleya Mntungwa, tell him someone once said change is the only constant in life.

Fred Khumalo Mathanda Ncube On a point of exigency, Madame Speaker, Fred admits he is new on Twitter, having started tweeting only in 2010 (you can check his profile). Yes, he doesn't tweet because he is long-winded and Twitter is all for brevity. But, in his defence, My Lady, Fred Khumalo watches what ppl gifted in brevity are saying on Twitter.

Phakamile Buthelezi I do believe though that Twitter is a lousy rip off of Facebook. Worse, Twitter users can be so ungovernable as they tend to share poor content on a regular basis. Twitter has falsely claimed 80% of celebs died.

Obed Mazwi I've had a Twitter account for over a year but I still don't know how to tweet...

Sipho Masondo About a month ago or so Sithe Msomi commented that old Robbie is there to cause hysteria every morning. I fully agree with him, NOW. The more I listen to the guy the more I ask myself just why on earth is he hosting a breakfast show. I heard that Twitter comment and immediately switched to SAfm. I'm tired of this howler.

Vanessa Perumal In deference to my profession I am gonna plead the fifth amendment on this BUT so glad this dialogue is articulated outside my quiet moments in my brain.

Zamuxolo Monwabisi Jimlongo Can all of us please come together and buy Robbie an economy class ticket to Ireland?

Me, me, me!

They don't know the name of Nelson Mandela's favourite dog ('If you can't google it, then it doesn't exist, LOL'). They can't spell ('That is so wack; it's for BBTs – born before technology'). They think Boom Boom Mancini is a Boom Shaka wannabe ('He must consider a new moniker if he wants to sell albums that we can readily recognise'). They frown uncomprehendingly when you tell them about Pandelani Nefolovhodwe's contribution to the anti-apartheid struggle ('With a name like that, it's no surprise he is a spent force,' they snigger).

By the time they are ten, their collection of personal portraits would put to shame any king or queen from seventeenth-century Europe, who at most had maybe four portraits and three sculptures in their palaces. The same monarch would squirm with envy to learn that these people also have gazillions of 'followers' on something called the internet.

Meet my children and their friends: AKA the Me Me Me Generation; AKA the Lazy Ones; AKA the Fidgety Fingers on the Fone Ones (which is only for texting and surfing the net. Return calls? That's so b4 Obama). When you speak to them – if you can corner them in their undies or pyjamas before they venture out of the house – they will only half-listen to you as they play with their ubiquitous devices, checking out who is 'liking' their status or retweeting their tweets. They are so nervous about being left behind that they constantly have to know what's 'trending' – especially if their names are tagged in the conversation.

Ah, these creatures are narcissistic.

However, before we start arguing about who exactly I am talking about here, let's establish the broader definitions of the generations that have preceded this lot – the group that some in South Africa have called the Born Frees. Personally, I don't like this term because it is politically loaded. It is also quite limited, based on the assumption that the world revolves around the problems this country experienced before 1994. Instead, I would like to broaden the net so as to position these people within a larger global context, in a period both before and after 1994. To augment my argument and draw my comparisons, it is inevitable that I will use sociological terminology that originated in the United States, since their academia has done so much research into social trends. Nevertheless, I will try to place these definitions within a local context as well.

We will start with the Lost Generation. These were the people born between 1883 and 1900 who were so named because they grew up in crushing poverty before being hit hard later by the Great Depression of the late 1920s and 1930s. In South Africa, these would have been people affected by the last Anglo-Zulu War, the Second Anglo-Boer War and World War I, as well as the Great Depression.

The baby boomers were born in the suburbs between 1943 and 1960. In America, they became yuppies who lost fortunes in the stock-market crash of 1987. Generation X – the term immortalised in Douglas Coupland's eponymous novel, published in 1991 – followed the baby boomers. Born between 1961 and 1980, they were the restless generation, never satisfied with their lot in life.[1]

While these definitions come from the US, they can apply to some extent to other developed countries, as well as developing countries such as South Africa, where they mostly pertain to white people. (Within a local context, studies such as these hardly ever scratch the surface of black lives.) There were certainly Generation

Xers who were prevalent in the white community in South Africa – youngsters who began to question things; who refused to be enlisted in the army; who wanted to know why black people were treated as they were back then. In the black community, the likes of Tsietsi Mashinini, who shot to prominence during the June 16 uprising, would be a perfect representative of this generation, too: selfless and committed to the common good of the community.

And then the millennials, the generation I have chosen to talk about, came along and changed it all. Born between 1980 and 2000 (hence the reference to the millennium), these youngsters are truly a global phenomenon. Members of this generation, be they in China, the US, Nigeria or South Africa, tend to have the same worldview as many of their peers in other parts of the world. Technology, of course, is the factor unifying them, the thing that sets them apart from previous generations. They obtain their values from the lessons spewed on MTV, Twitter, Facebook, Myspace and all the other platforms mushrooming all over the place. They rap, they swag.

Their home language could be Igbo, Mandarin, Twi, Zulu, Amharic; but the language that is common to all of them is Me Me Me – the holy trinity of Me, Myself and I. These are the people who will tweet while sitting on a toilet moaning about their irregular bowel movements. They will Facebook a picture of the lunch they are having. Born in the shadow of reality TV, they are themselves stars in their own reality shows. They derive satisfaction from being celebrities – even though they are only celebrated by themselves and their egos, or by their circle of 'friends'.

And yet the reality in which they 'interact' with this endless stream of 'friends' is a false one. How many times have you seen three or four of these creatures walk into an eating establishment, sit down to a meal and get down to thumbing their phones? Thirty, forty minutes later, when they have finished eating, they have not uttered a single word to each other! Having a meal with friends used to be about sharing an experience, commenting on the food or the décor of the restaurant.

Then there is reading, which is another concept unfamiliar to them. While millennials certainly seem to have figured out the letters of the alphabet, as proven in their frequent use of OMG, WTF, BTW, you can't really call that reading or writing. If you really want to drive them berserk, lock them inside a library stocked with a wealth of books and newspaper clippings, give them a computer minus the internet, and ask them to write a properly referenced two-thousand-word essay about 'The Meaning of Obama' or, better still, 'What Lady Gaga Means to Me', or 'Why I Relate Better to Lindiwe Mazibuko than Julius Malema'.

With such a wealth of information at their fingertips, however, many millennials probably feel that having to do such research is completely unnecessary. I quote from the *Time* magazine article which inspired me to write about this phenomenon in the first place: 'The Industrial Revolution made individuals far more powerful – they could move to a city, start a business, read and form organisations. The information revolution has further empowered individuals by handing them the technology to compete against the huge organisations: hackers vs corporations; bloggers vs newspapers.'[2]

Yep, the millennials don't need us, and that's why we are scared of them. There, I said it. But before you whoop with joy, you tjat-jarag narcissist, let me tell you what I've just done: I have quoted something that I read and attributed it accordingly. The technology generation has neither the patience nor the humility to acknowledge sources. I've lost count of the occasions when these creatures have stolen my words and put them on their Facebook pages, or even used them in their academic essays without acknowledging that one Fred Khumalo sweated bullets in order to come up with those shimmering nuggets of prose.

This is also not to say that I don't take advantage of the tools that have made this generation what they are. I tweet, I Facebook, I podcast, I YouTube, I blog and I utilise all the other things in between, because I am in the communication business. Technology is a means to an end. But to some of these millennial creatures, the mantra is: 'I tweet (or Facebook), therefore I am.' Technology becomes an end in itself.

For the record, I wrote this piece in one sitting without touching my phone or flipping the screen to my Facebook page. While doing so, what did I miss, what did I miss? Where the party at, my niggas? Is Rihanna back with Chris Brown? Has Khanyi Mbau added another layer of flesh to her lips? Has Malema unfriended me?

Sunday World, 18 June 2013

Speaking in tongues

'Why do people hate on North West?' That's right. I had to do a double take before I could make sense of that headline in the *Huffington Post*. Apparently, what it really means is: 'Why do people hate North West?' – North West in this case being Kanye West and Kim Kardashian's daughter. I know we mangle the Queen's tongue every day, but pleez maaan: 'Why do you hate on me?' And when I raise this with my kids ('kids' being children, I'm not a goat!), they always roll their eyes and say, 'Ah, Dad, get with the programme. That's how we roll these days. Don't hate on us.'

Facebook, 20 November 2014

Bhekisisa Mncube These people are full of beans in a Zulu kinda way. Singathi nje bashipha ubhotshisi. [We could simply say they are farting beans.] Don't judge me on my Zulu.

Phil Mhlongo Haters gonna hate potatoes gonna potate!

Khomotso Naka Ntate Khumalo, hating 'on' someone and hating someone are two different things.

Doreen Gough The cold blooded murder of the English tongue.

Fred Khumalo Educate me, Khomotso Naka.

Fred Khumalo I am waiting Khomotso Naka. 'On' is generally a preposition. What purpose does it serve here? One never runs away from a pedagogical opportunity. So, I'm all ears ...

Khomotso Naka Hating someone is having intense dislike for that individual. Hating on someone on the other hand is like what you might call 'u ku ba ne kwali' ['having a dislike for someone'] (excuse my isiZulu).

Khomotso Naka You need a different mindset to understand this. Proper English grammar does not apply here.

Fred Khumalo So let's rather confine this to English, Khomotso Naka, because I don't understand what you mean by 'kwali' and Zulu is my mother tongue. I am waiting for my education. Maybe 'hating on someone' is, like, 'mild hatred'? Is that the sentiment? Grammatically, it still doesn't cut the mustard. But hey, don't hate on me, I always want to make sure I have a full understanding of a phrase before I use it.

Khomotso Naka Urban dictionary definition: v. To be jealous of another's success or talent. Note that the person being hated on must possess these qualities. So while the child in question possesses neither success nor talent, I'm guessing that it is her wealth and heritage that is being 'hated on'.

Khomotso Naka Beyond this ntate I cannot help.

Fred Khumalo Great, Khomotso Naka. So it's already in the Urban Dictionary! I wonder who aggregates this Urban Dictionary and how often they have to change, since these new words probably fall by the wayside to be replaced by others in a few months (you don't have to respond; this old man is just musing to himself). Okay, Doreen Gough and other fossils like myself, now you know this is the urban truth, Ruth.

Khomotso Naka Pheew!!

Zimasa Ntuli It's like saying, 'Drink up!' or 'He won't live it down'. We say these things just because it feels good to say them.

Fan these fragrant winds of change

Michelle Obama had no sooner finished her address at Soweto's Regina Mundi Church during the Obamas' visit to South Africa in September 2009 before the peacetime revolutionaries of the republic began to wonder aloud: 'Why do we need an American to inspire us? What are these Americans trying to extract from our country now? They must go back home and fix their own shit. We need African solutions for African problems. Blah blah.'

Cynical as I am about the so-called American Dream – a moribund proposition which holds that you can only partake of the benefits of a society if you can pull yourself up by your bootstraps (what if you don't have the boots to start with?) – I still found myself inspired by Obama's down-to-earth address, which, contrary to what the peacetime revolutionaries have said, did not try to offer solutions for this country. Rather, it reminded us that we hold our destiny in our own hands and have the potential to realise our collective dream as South Africans.

When I was a young boy, my maternal grandma used to tell us a story about a mythical snake that was short-sighted and paranoid. At the slightest crackle of twigs in the forest, it would start thrashing about, trying to bite an imaginary enemy. Finding none, it would then begin devouring itself, first its tail and then the rest of its body. Believing it had enemies all over the place, the snake preferred to harm itself rather than wait to see what its imagined foes were going to do to it.

Maybe it's too harsh an analogy, but I find that South African society has become so increasingly myopic that the slightest rustle in the forest inspires us to run for cover or to lash out at our enemies in anger, all because we won't allow anyone to tell us how we should deal with the challenges we face here.

We might be divided into various racial or political cliques – white, black, coloured, Indian; the ANC, the DA, the FF+ – but, collectively, we are united in our touchiness, our self-righteousness, and our downright myopia and paranoia.

Each collective has gone further by surrendering its fate to a particular leader. What makes things worse is that the leaders suffer from a bad case of halitosis, which we love them for nonetheless. At first we suspected that this leadership halitosis was bad, but with time we have become hypnotised. The halitosis is the glue, after all, that keeps us together; the divine plan that makes sure our individual cliques keep chugging along.

So when a stranger ventures into our part of the forest and starts fanning her nose in disgust, we are equally disgusted with the stranger. How dare she suggest that our leadership or our ideas stink?

None of this, however, has stopped me from feeling like I have been roused from the stupor inspired by our leaders' halitosis, especially after Michelle Obama said, 'You can be the generation that brings opportunity and prosperity to forgotten corners of the world and banishes hunger from this continent forever; you can be the generation that teaches the world that HIV is fully preventable and treatable, and should never be a source of shame; you can be the generation that holds your leaders accountable for open, honest government at every level, government that stamps out corruption and protects the rights of every citizen to speak freely, to worship openly, to love whomever they choose.'[1]

Unlike the reek of halitosis that permeates the declarations of the smelly local leadership, Obama's words were laden with the scent of jasmine, with a reminder that I, as a citizen of South Africa, have the potential to do some good for my country, in whatever small measure.

In the vulnerable period when a country is rebuilding itself from the foundations upward, just as in times of war, bellicosity can easily become a new religion. Intellectual midgets, agile and wily as they tend to be, become the high priests of this faith. And these midgets are, invariably, the individuals who are perched on the seats of leadership so you can't question them. You have to imbibe their halitosis, help to spread it around; let it become the national, racial, cultural or organisational perfume.

Their rallying slogans go something like: 'The leaders say our liberal party with a proud English-speaking tradition can't be dictated to by Afrikaners; the leaders say we must nationalise this and nationalise that,' and so on. When a stranger, or some deluded dreamer who is immune to the national or cultural halitosis, points out that we should at least try to run existing parastatals competently and get government departments to deliver on their mandate and promises, or that we should cover the toilets that we are dispensing to the poor, all before we actually consider nationalising, the dreamer in question is usually smothered with generous fumes of our national or organisational halitosis until he or she shuts up.

It is also not as if we never had thinkers and visionaries in this country before Michelle Obama arrived here. We had them in the past; we still have them now. Figures such as Albertina Sisulu and her husband Walter, both of whom worked for years towards building communities and putting children who were not theirs into school, and who never sought praise or attention for their deeds. Even Nelson Mandela was cajoled into entering higher education by Sisulu, although not many of our leaders know that.

Kader Asmal was another visionary. Yes, he had many flaws, including an annoying pomposity and self-righteousness, but the man was driven by a dream of building an ideal, egalitarian, enquiring, educated and responsible South African citizenry. He spoke out against the excesses of government, the rising thuggery of the ANC he so loved; he raised his hand in objection to the Protection of Information Bill.

Unlike many of the leaders riding this gravy train which Asmal criticised, both he and the Sisulus lived simple, unadorned lifestyles and were not complainers. The same cannot be said of many of our current leaders who see a pot of gold at the end of every political or public office endeavour.

Needless to say, the Sisulus and the Asmals of this world, owing to their long service to the struggle, are almost begrudgingly beyond reproach from the intellectual midgets. But unfortunately for South Africans, there are other dreamers and visionaries who do not have the same public profiles as the Sisulus and Asmal. And when these individuals choose to raise their voices every now and then, we have to find it within ourselves to nurture and support them. As they tend to think before they talk, that moment of reflection, that moment when they pause is considered a weakness. They are deemed indecisive. The intellectual tokoloshes, on the other hand, the ones spanning both the racial and political divide, blurt out things quickly and easily without thinking. And, alas, it is their half-baked pronouncements masquerading as thoughts which find fertile ground in the hearts and minds of a desperate and largely uneducated and unsophisticated citizenry.

We inhale their halitosis in huge gulps as if it were a life-giving gas. Perhaps it is life-giving, because when we are denied this halitosis and are exposed to the jasmine scent of Obama's words our bodies get confused. 'What is this American woman saying, telling us we can be good? We don't want to be good, we want to defeat the enemy!' Whoever that enemy is. Halitosis-inspired myopia reigns supreme.

So when she tells us how, after graduating from Harvard Law School, she got a job at a fancy law firm – nice salary, big office – we nod in awe and admiration.

But when she says that she looked around her neighbourhood and saw broken families, uneducated people, semi-skilled people who couldn't find jobs, and that this inspired her to quit her cushy job so she could train young people for careers in public service – even though this meant she wasn't earning as much money as she used to – suddenly we feel uncomfortable.

She didn't work so hard at university in order to be poor, surely? That's the rhetoric we are used to: we didn't struggle to be poor.

But it is these kinds of utterances from powerful people such as Michelle Obama that remind us of the potential we have as a nation – of the sacrifices we have made in the past to defeat apartheid, and the long road and future sacrifices ahead as we now take on the not-so-fancy task of rebuilding our nation. You can demolish an edifice in a few hours, but building a new one is more demanding. This will require planning, resources and sheer doggedness.

Therefore, let us cultivate more Michelle Obamas so that we can be continuously reminded to keep our eye on the ball.

Come on. We can do better than to capitulate and be slaves to the whims of the butchers and murderers of this country's hopes and dreams, the halitotic spectres who call themselves our leaders.

TimesLive, 16 September 2009

Conducting research at the gym, Somizi Mhlongo style

I went to the gym the other day after a long hiatus. It had been such a long break that I had forgotten the habits of my fellow gymgoers.

Back at the Morningside branch of Virgin Active, I smiled to myself as I spotted all the familiar faces that had coloured my previous gym experiences. The white guy who wears the really, really tight-fitting wife beater with the track pants, baseball cap and sunglasses was still there. He is noticeable for never getting down to the real business of being inside a gym – you know, exercising.

No, he prances about so we can admire his bulk, which is quite impressive, I must admit. To look at his face, the fellow must be in his late sixties, yet his muscles are still firm. Unfortunately, at that age you never can win the battle against the bulge. So the naughty eye forgets about his impressive physique only to concentrate on his awkward oversized belly which stands out no matter how much he sucks it in.

In this man's never-ending inspection of the gym he finds time to pause every now and again to give advice to a total stranger like myself. 'I can see you are trying to do a dead-lift but your posture is all wrong,' he will say. Then he will usurp the weights from me so he can demonstrate how it's really done – only to realise the weights I have packed are too heavy.

'The weighting here is excessive, all wrong,' he remonstrates, 'that's why your posture gets compromised, which in turn will mess up your back. And once your back is messed up, many other things will get messed up, too.' Wink wink, nudge nudge.

When he first did this some time ago, I told him to mind his own business. This time around, however, I was so overwhelmed with nostalgia that I simply shrugged and watched him as he taught me how to lift.

There's also the woman who, when lifting weights, cries out as if she's having the orgasm of a lifetime. The less said about her, the better.

Another gym eccentric is Somizi Mhlongo. I used to see him a lot at the Old Eds branch of Virgin Active. Whenever I catch sight of him, dressed in a skimpy little number that looks like a panty, he would also be prancing all over the floor. Not once did I actually witness him engaged in physical exertions.

This picture of an almost-naked Somizi used to assail my mind even when I was in the US in 2011. Unlike Somizi, the guys at Harvard did not like being seen naked in the communal shower area.

While people in South Africa prance about freely in their naked glory, exhibiting all shapes and sizes of male tools and buttocks, the denizens at the Harvard gym which I used to go to are really very private when it comes to their privates. Their actions used to have me wondering whether the American male species was more reserved or introverted than their African counterparts – an unfair generalisation, of course, seeing that Harvard, an international cauldron of cultures and nationalities, does not represent the whole of America.

However, it is remarkable to see the lengths that these men would go to in order to hide those areas of their anatomy from others. At Harvard, a guy comes sweating from the gym area, gets into the communal shower area where he sheds his top, pants and shoes, and then goes to the private shower cubicle in his underwear with a towel in hand. When he comes out of the shower, he is wrapped in his towel before discreetly sliding into a fresh pair of underwear without removing the towel. As he does this, he keeps stealing furtive glances around him to make sure that no one catches even a glimpse of his buttocks.

These mannerisms not only had me sniggering but made me think that Somizi Mhlongo would be highly offended. What were these men at Harvard trying to hide? I can't imagine that a professorial spear would be any different from an MBA *mshini wami*, so why make it a mystery? We are all men. These matters need to be aired in public.

Some of you will ask the obvious question: why drag Somizi into this? I would answer that it's simply because I enjoy looking at Somizi looking at naked guys.

Of course, I do all these observations in the name of research. As a journalist and a novelist I have to observe people at close quarters. Who knows, for my next novel I might be inspired to create a scene that takes place inside the male showers at a gym. And when describing the mannerisms of men in their natural habitat I will have to be as accurate as possible. We call it verisimilitude – realism in the world of writing.

I am sure Somizi also watches these guys in the name of research. As a choreographer he is trained to admire bodies, to keep thinking: 'That body over there could be moulded into a brilliant dancer, if only he could give me the opportunity to train him.'

Now that I am back at the gym, maybe I should do away with my shyness and collaborate with Somizi on a book/video combination. We could call it *Magic at the Gym Showers*.

Could be fireworks, darrrling!

Sowetan, 4 March 2016

Zithulele Sibanyoni This woman. You know, the one you dedicated all of one sentence to in your narrative, Fred Khumalo. Is she black or white? I'm thinking of taking up a Virgin Active subscription myself, for research of course.

Fred Khumalo Hahaha, Zithulele Sibanyoni we don't allow perverts at my gym, you know. But the lady in question is of the Caucasian persuasion.

Zithulele Sibanyoni Oh OK. I was asking for a friend anyway.

Shaheed JazzGuy Farred I think there is an extremely unfair advantage in the men's room in favour of gay guys.......You sometimes catch them staring around the shower cubicles.

Musa Sibandze What I get is that your deadlift is heavy. Everyone has an ego. Even you. LOL

Fred Khumalo You got my ego figured out! You are so smart! Give this man a Bells!

Tshire Kau OMG an O— of a lifetime.

Fred Khumalo Come, now, Tshire. What's an O.... of a lifetime? We don't beat about the bush, here. We air things out in the open. Come!

Siyanda Ndawo And he says 'come!'

Brenda Wardle Fred you have me stitches but hey ndiyasola [I am suspicious]. I must trek back to Virgin Active. I had an admirer there who used to grunt like a strangled goat when he was on the treadmill but times were brighter then as I was in a relationship so we would both be entertained. I think Maboni Mthiyane used to gym with you so I know all about your yadda yadda disguised in a vest.

Lebogang Thobye Research can make you do things, hey Fred Khumalo? Just watch you don't get misunderstood.

Masivuye Pototo Sangoni I have never laughed so much. It reminds of your writings in the Sunday Times.

Gail Wannenburg Ha ha.

Solly Moeng Joh!

Charmz Ma Soeu Made me LOL.

Kota Nomfanelo Pun unintended ...I love u Fred Khumalo.... Bua!

Milandru Dennis Mapengo LOL. Laughter 4 a Jozi mornin.

Solomon Smonds Nomonde Bab'Mntungwa, were they black or white men? If they were black I'd be very disappointed bcos that would 'shatter' my fantasies. I always fantasise of meeting this tall, well-hung black man 4rm the States. Didn't they originate 4rm West Africa? The Kunta Kintes? They r supposed 2 be 'extra-endowed', with rippling muscles & tight bums... There, I'm fantasising again...!

Veronica Mohapeloa So it means u go around the shower naked?

Ziningi Nkosi LOL

Abel-Goitsemang 'Tsitsi' Mogotsi lmao..Fred, lol..i would b offended if Somizi stares at my nakedness.

Mpho Vida Koma Lmao! Ya neh..!! U jus killed me this morning Mr Khumalo!! Lol!

Lukhanyo Vuyo L Mbande It's possible that the emergence of folks who find others of similar gender attractive may be the motivating factor in being secretive, I have been also made to feel uncomfortable when I visit gymnasiums around Cape Town, one feels violated when you see someone devouring your behind, this behaviour has made me argue that maybe it's time that we stop having these communal showers, of course in my village being naked in front of other men has never been an issue but now the world has changed dramatically and we need to adapt.

David Muir You are correct in your observations: but it is in fact a relatively new phenomenon, they say, which has developed over the last 20–30 years. At Stanford, where I was, some guys showered in their underwear, then went into cubicles to change. Bizarre. Many high schools now do not even have showers, apparently, since they are not used. The new prudery has been attributed to various things, such as the growth of the Christian right and the gay rights movement (which forced men to realise that there were !gasp! men around who might enjoy seeing them naked). I notice the same tendencies here now, even to the ridiculous extent that guys get changed under their towels just as you notice there!

Heather Lewis You have been away from Africa for too long now if this problem is giving you an epiphany.

Sello Molefe This makes a great chapter for your next book. Please call it 'Coming in America'.

Moses Maseko Hey Fred, thanks for this eye-opener. What do you think informs that mentality & attitude amongst the Americans? It'd be interesting to know!

Heather Lewis Well (this is a comment from a total outsider as I have never been near America and I need a break from standing on a ladder pruning the ivy), but it could be to do with raising little boys to be ashamed of their bodies. Research is needed here: how do naked American females behave in the showers?

David Muir @Lukhanyo: your interesting observation deserves comment. I am a gay man and not a shy one either, but I remain very aware that inappropriate behaviour can and will make other people uncomfortable and no one has the right to do that. So no, I don't spend my time in the locker room ogling. However, it also has to be said that straight men are often hypersensitive on this issue: it may betray a prejudice that is more linked to 'ignorance of the other' than anything else, and to close down locker rooms or start behaving in inhibited ways because of imagined behaviours in others would be very sad. I have straight friends that I shower with or swim with who don't give a damn that I am with them (without the blindfold, too – they let me stop wearing that quite a while ago). This goes to the heart of the issue that gay and straight men need to talk and interact more: neither group is going away anytime soon.

Dennis Morton Hmmmmm cock shy syndrome or do black men have larger dicks?

Sindi Lingela They are afraid of uMntungwa omkhulu [the great Mntungwa].

Brenda Wardle Goodness I see we have had our coffee black, strong with a dash of testosterone this morning. This is right up Eddie Murphy's alley. Can't help but wonder what Obama's Harvard Locker Room Review would read like. That definitely ain't no shy nigger.

Mvusiwekhaya Sicwetsha Hahaha. Do you picture Juju joining the imperialists in the shower, reacting to their attempt to hide their glory?

Brenda Wardle Mvusiwekhaya why do I get the distinct feeling Juju would not share Fred's sentiments? The cheeks maybe?

Mvusiwekhaya Sicwetsha Hahhaha. Let him answer for himself. Let's just say, people are protective. I also used to wrap myself with my towel in my old gym. You will never know these days, with the rise of homes. It's better to be safe than sorry.

David Muir @Anita. In a locker room you want privacy?

David Muir Also, I have to say, these straight men who claim they have to protect themselves from those dreadful pervy 'homes' lusting after them should probably consider that they have dreams WAY above their station. Dudes we could give a shit.

Fred Khumalo Veronica Mohapeloa, of course I do walk around naked in the communal locker room area of the gym. That's what guys do back home – both black and white.

Fred Khumalo Heather Lewis If I had my way, I would embark on that research of checking out American female behaviour in the locker room. But, I guess, the system doesn't allow me to venture into that territory.

Fred Khumalo And, people, before this communication gets distorted, let me remind you that in my original post, I did note that the Harvard community is NOT representative of America. Harvard is the United Nations with a pedagogical bent.

Fred Khumalo David is correct, the more those of us who are straight spent more time with gay guys, the more we will realise how unfounded our fears/prejudices/misconceptions are. Matters of sexuality (like matters of culture/race are the well-spring of many misconceptions and phobias). Not so long ago in South Africa – and this is still applicable to vast swathes of our community – people from diverse racial/cultural backgrounds had misconceptions about each other. But once you have crossed the racial/cultural divide you suddenly realise how foolish we all have been about confining ourselves to our respective laagers, and pointing fingers at those outside the laager. The classical US and THEM narrative.

Heather Lewis With Fred's writing skills he should manage to rustle up a grant to investigate all pedagogical locker rooms as part of an equal opportunity research programme.

No 'darkie' sarcasm
in the class struggle

A friend of mine was having a late lunch at one of those popular family-food franchises when he witnessed something that made him do a double take: two tables away from him, a family of six were eating sandwiches that they had brought with them in a plastic container strategically placed on the seat away from the waitress's line of vision.

To cover up their culinary hoard, the family had bought a round of cold drinks and a huge plate of chips. And when they thought no one was watching, the mother would plunge a hand into the container and fish out a sandwich, surreptitiously passing it to one of her charges, who would wolf it down quickly and pick up a chip for good measure.

These were not hobos, by the way. They were clean and well groomed. There was even a bunch of car keys on the table. When the waitress came back and asked, 'Anything else for you folk?', the matriarch responded: 'Not yet, thank you.'

Much later, when the waitress came back again, one of the children – who must have been about seven – blurted out: 'But Mommy said she was taking us to a restaurant and all she's doing is feeding us sangwidges from home! Mommy, ask the lady here to give us some syrup at least. The sangwidges are dry!'

When I repeated the story to a group of new friends they laughed themselves silly. That is, until I came to the post-punchline punchline: 'You know, I thought smuggling food or drinks into a restaurant was a darkie thing. Only darkies can get away with that kind of thing, not you people.'

Silence around the table. You see, four of the six people present were white, and only one of them was a bosom buddy who is familiar with my stories; the others were strangers who had been enthusiastically introduced to the man my friend had described as this 'writer, you'll find him interesting'. The family I'd been telling the story about was white, too.

Realising my faux pas, I excused myself and went to the toilet. My friend got up to join me. 'My bad,' I said to her. 'Seems like I've got your friends upset. I thought they were the kind of people who're just like you, you know, open-minded and all. But, what can I say, the story is true. The family was white.'

'That is not what upset them,' she said to me.

'Then what?'

'That ugly word,' she said, 'which I've asked you not to use in the company of strangers.'

The penny dropped: I had used the word darkie! A few of my best friends – make that 'white friends' – always feel mightily uncomfortable when I use that word.

Nevertheless, I could sense that this present crowd's discomfort stemmed not just from that word but from the very mention of race. In the circles I move in it has suddenly become tricky to talk about the issue. Race has become an elephant in the room. We know it is there, we can sense its presence, yet we avert our eyes and pretend it's just the colour of the curtains that makes the room dark and stuffy. It's the elephant, people! The race elephant.

One silly friend of mine, who happens to be black, said the conversation now should be about class, not race. I'll have you know this, brother: race, in this country, is still by and large a class determinant.

It is no accident that the majority of the people who are poor are black. A racial oligarchy designed it that way. To change the class situation, you will need to educate and empower the majority – a project that will take maybe another century, or even more, to realise fully.

Just because you and I live in the suburbs and hang out with white people who earn the same salaries as we do, does not mean that our reality defines that of the rest of the South African populace. The gap between rich and poor is still driven, largely, by race. There are white people who didn't have to raise a finger to find themselves smack in the lap of luxury. They were born into it. Race determined their class situation.

The blacks who are drinking whiskies, the names of which they can't even pronounce, are telling us to forget about race while conveniently overlooking this: they are part of the middle class thanks to affirmative action. In other words: because of race.

When I shared this observation with the friend I had embarrassed by using the word 'darkie' in polite white company, she objected to my equating poverty with blackness: 'What about all these black millionaires that we read about in the papers?'

Exactly my point. You read about them in the papers because they are a novelty, not the norm. How many thousands of multimillionaires are in this country that you don't even know about because they are white? Is this not another way of equating wealth with whiteness: that it is normal to be white and rich, and therefore nothing to write home about?

The handful of new black billionaires in South Africa hasn't changed the reality of the millions of other black people in this country who live in abject poverty, nor does it imply that race no longer determines one's station in this country. According to Statistics South Africa, in 2011 about 20.2 per cent of the black population lived below the food poverty line of R321 a person a month. The black population was the most severely affected by poverty in general, with 54 per cent living under the poverty line.[1]

One extremely obese Khulubuse Zuma does not a contented black South Africa make.

It's dangerous to pretend that things are normal, that people of all colours can pull themselves up by their bootstraps. Most of these people do not even have the boots to start with. That's why it becomes kind of acceptable for darkies to smuggle food and drinks into restaurants: they want to create an air of normality in a situation that is painfully abnormal.

Mail & Guardian, 13 June 2014

Exalt Interesting article. I would have liked you to explain a little more of what you think the solution is? I think everyone agrees in South Africa race is still synonymous with class. However, you seem to have some internal conflict over whether you are a product of AA or whether that's just for rich blacks. I believe you got to write such good articles on account of your own value and not on account of a racist policy. By your own account then, this policy is not the answer. We need to empower black people in South Africa, to get the boots, the straps and the willpower to pull them up. In terms of education, in terms of a thriving private sector, in terms of a healthy macroeconomic environment. I think the problem most people have when dealing with this issue is to think a complex problem will be solved with a simple solution. Not enough rich blacks? Legislate wealth to blacks! It doesn't work like that and as unpopular as that is, we need to acknowledge the breadth of the problem in front of us. We need to work together to build the staircase to wealth for all. As long as we cling ashamedly to this thing called race and continue to implement 'low road' policies, we will never find those solutions and South Africa's dream will become a nightmare again. I dearly hope it won't take us 100 years from democracy to realise that. Time waits for no man my friend... 20 years and counting by the way...

Hopeful Thanks for the story, this whitie would have roared with laughter. I agree it is the elephant Fred, let's bring it up and bring it out! There are some things you guys do great, and there are some things us guys do great. And the obverse. Let's talk about it. To answer the second part, the only transformation that works in my opinion, is education, in an economy that is NOT socialist – by all means do an aggressive wealth transfer, but leave people alone to work. All this takes good teachers, and decades. Has anyone noticed that the next US presidential Republican candidate might be a genuine African American, from genuinely poor origins? Dr Ben Carson, who gets right up Pres. Obama's nose.

Mish14 As a long term visitor to your country, I found this article expresses some of what I have observed during my time here. The degree to which everyday events in South Africa are racialised by the local population is beyond anything I have experienced before. It is something that I am trying to understand, and welcome local perspectives on the situation. I imagine that the history of apartheid IS a large contributing factor. While some will say 'It's been 20 years', in the grand scheme of societal change, that is still a very small period of time. I agree that poverty is experienced across races and cultures, but the hangover from apartheid's oppression of groups of people is certainly still keenly felt today. The ANC also needs to take responsibility for not making the most of the opportunities they have had, and continue to have in markedly changing mindsets. Instead, they have too often reinforced divisive and damaging outlooks, which is a huge barrier to the progress that is possible if they would govern honorably.

Pierre Aycard You write: 'The increase in the number of visibly wealthy blacks does not change the fact that race still determines one's station in life in this country.'
I believe you are slightly mistaken: the increase in the number of

black billionaires is changing things a lot, for the worst. For two reasons: firstly, because the poor now believe things are fine, because some blacks can become rich, famous and powerful. This way the poor do not always see the need to keep asking for change. Rather, they get lured. Secondly, because many of those black billionaires also got rich by doing nothing. Within the Mandela and Zuma families (for instance), guys were given ownership of mining companies (among others), not for their merit, but for that of their fathers. And those guys have no shame forgetting to pay their (Black and White) workers for months or years, while spreading their lavish and insulting lifestyle in the face of the poor.

The problem fundamentally, is not race, but as you rightfully point out, everybody acts like it is, like a bad habit they could never shake off. The rich and average-rich whites don't see and don't know anything more today than they used to yesterday. The poor know and see far less than they used to: because there is no more political education given to them; because they see some actual achievements rather than all that should have been achieved further and wasn't; and because they would rather see any black leader tell them everything is alright, than treat a crooked black leader like they once were ready to treat crooked white leaders.

It is time for all, Blacks and Whites, to meditate the words of Steve Biko, who tried to free people, whether they were green, purple or blue: 'Being black is a matter of where you stand in the capitalist-colonial system of domination'.

That means blackness is neither in you skin, nor in your poverty: it is in one's inability to understand that one is treated as a slave. It is in the fact that one becomes and remains an accomplice of one's own condition of slavery.

The rich (Whites mainly, but not only) must understand that they are slaves to their own choices too, hiding themselves in gated cloisters; living between home, the office, the car and the mall; preparing the crisis that will cause their fall. And the poor (Blacks mainly, but clearly not only) must understand that only oneself can free oneself.

And again you are right in your article: real change will start when everyone is free to talk about race with anyone, and to laugh about it. Then minds will find room to address the real issue. I experienced Cape Town and UCT, where the rich don't understand much, despite their smart looks. I experienced the deepest Soweto, where Blacks don't understand much either, despite their pride at having once led a revolution.

Time for those who understand to come out of the woods, to bite, and thus to transmit the virus of awareness...

stuzaza Usually i enjoy this writer's slant on things, Not today. Sub Saharan Africa is not a well developed region – western Europe is. The trajectories toward 'first world' status of these two regions were and are totally different. Left alone without outside influence one wonders what kind of place Africa would be today? 'Race determines ones station' is absolute bollocks. Class, as a social construct, will always exist. Any stats this writer spews are indicative not of oligarchical dominance but of demographic breakdown and are, therefore, meaningless as an attempt to reason the apparent inequalities. Further, one only has to look at western Europe vs eastern Europe, for example, to see very similar forces at play. Africa is not unique. Peoples that can educate themselves will thrive – those that sit back, wallow in the sick injustices of the world and blame 'da man' deserve their station. Africa has never been at the forefront of positive world achievement – why should we expect anything different, in a hurry, now? Hiding this fact behind some BS oppression sob story is just stupid. Oh and drop the 'darkie' references and friends 'who happen to be black' – it just perpetuhates race in a country where PEOPLE need to connect with PEOPLE.

Frank Lee Fred, blacks live in poverty for the same reason that in years gone by, most of Europe lived in poverty while the aristocracy lived in opulence. It is an accident of birth.

History has shown that you can huff and puff all you like about the injustice of it all, but you are probably better off by just rolling up your sleeves and creating your own wealth instead of trying to rectify the accident of birth.

Who said life should be fair?

African Knight If there were no white people in South Africa, would the black people be any better off? The answer is no, if all the whites were ordered out tomorrow like Idi Amin in Uganda initially there would be a few more blacks (usually the connected ones) with a few more assets but the initial euphoria would give way to a grim reality that Africa will be asset rich but economically poor. Hard work and entrepreneurship is the root out of poverty and the poor blacks don't have enough of it. No amount of class struggle crap is ever going to change any ground realities. The poor blacks are destined to stay poor.

Col Nyathi Good article Mntungwa but as black people I think we need to inculcate the spirit of honest and hard work. I sometimes get the feeling that some of our black people visualise government as this big Father Christmas who is there to just give. So if I am a young lady I can get pregnant and go to the local social service centre so government 'takes care of my child'. The same government 'should give us houses because we voted for them'.

The situation is not helped by youthful politicians who make it through the skewed tender processes. They also over-invoice government because this Father Christmas has money and then they have the guts to show-off.

We just need to introduce basic civic education so our youth understand responsibility and then we fix our education and then maybe in a shorter time we can have a different picture.

Bantu Education, I love you!

Okay, friends, it's time for one of those bizarre Fred Khumalo conversations. I am going to pose one question, for a start, in what I hope will be a long discussion. For reasons that shall soon become evident, I would like to restrict the earlier stages of this conversation to black South Africans who are over thirty-five and did not go to boarding school. In other words, I want the true products of Bantu Education to come forward. Now be a good egg and answer my question. Do not try to be a Clever Black and cheat. And *do not* google! Answer from the bottom of your heart. When did you first hear of or read about Hansel and Gretel? And what do you know about these characters?

Facebook, 17 November 2014

Respect Deejay Vernon Itjaaa......from this post I know nothing....
Mbambo Lindelani Never... yini leyo?
Fred Khumalo Ah, that's the spirit, Respect Deejay Vernon and Mbambo Lindelani. Noted.
Khuli Sisanda Seyisi A few years ago when my children would tell me about the stories read at nursery school. Later we went to see a theatre production during school holidays. Can't quite recall what it's all about but I think it's about two kids that got lost, something something.
Fred Khumalo Khuli Sisanda Seyisi, thanks for the honesty!

Sonwabile Ndamase My head is all over the show can't get it! Just assist and remind please!

Ramahetlane Ariel I have only seen the movie on Mnet and they are brother and sister killing witches!

Fred Khumalo Be patient, Sonwabile Ndamase. People are still sending in their submissions.

Fred Khumalo Aha, Ntholeng Ariel, that's right.

Nkosinathi Mzwamahlubi Myataza Colliers Encyclopedia we had at home.

Fred Khumalo Nkosinathi Mzwamahlubi Myataza, you even had an encyclopedia at home! Why do I get the feeling you do not qualify here. Please assume observer status!

Daluxolo Moloantoa Thought you were speaking about Hansa and Groschl. That's my closest guess.

Vulindlela S. Kunene Fictional characters created from fables by famed Danish author, Hans Christian Erikssen. My very model C primary school (am Swazi), brother and sister who got lost in the woods, brother's greed led to them eating a witch's house, witch caught them, wanted to spit-braai them, they escape, made witch pizza whilst doing so. The End.

Fred Khumalo Ah, Daluxolo Moloantoa, now there's my nigga. As for Vulindlela S. Kunene: your Model C school did not teach you very well. You don't listen: I specifically said South African blacks, product of Bantu Education, you tjatjarag Swazi agent! You're the weakest link. OUT.

Vulindlela S. Kunene Hehehe. #TucksTailInBetweenLegs #Leaves

Sima Majola Mncnm! I have always suspected that unobandlululo [you're discriminatory]. Why ungabuzanga [didn't you ask] into that will include the likes of me engayiswa eboarding school. Akubona utshwala lobu obuvela kuTV? [I who was sent to boarding school. Is this not booze being advertised on TV?]

Fred Khumalo I repeat: no boarding schools, no Model Cs, no whites,

no Indians. No Clever Blacks. Suiwer Bantoe Education products. I
want to see where this goes ...

Nelisa Ndondo Pitsi Mmmmmmmhhh kwanzima. Angikaze ngizwele
ngalezinto nakwamadala ejudeni. [Mmmmmmmhhh, this is tough.
I've never heard such, ever in my life.] *walks away*

Sithe Msomi Yes mina I knew Hansa when I finished high school and
started drinking. The other beer must have been created long after I
had graduated to Cognac.

Fred Khumalo Nelisa Ndondo Pitsi, you are not alone (in Michael
Jackson's voice).

Sima Majola You have just 'shredded' my heart. So Mandela was in jail
for this?

Luvuyo Mgolodela Who's that?

Fred Khumalo Dolus eventualis. Dolus ignoramus.

Fred Khumalo Vumani Mkhize, don't even open your mouth. You
don't qualify for this conversation....

Vumani Mkhize Hahaha, Fred. OK my mouth is sealed. But what do
you have against people who went to boarding school?

Lizo Cagwe Never heard of these characters. Will ask my children.

Fred Khumalo Lizo Cagwe, you're on the right track. Your children
should know.

S'bu Khoza Mmhh... I doubt any1 from Mpumalanga ikasi lami has an
answer to this.

Wynona Rose Eish Fred. I dont know if I qualify for this question....
went to CED school....but know the story from home not school. My
mom was a teacher.......(so what's your moral of your story?)

Fred Khumalo Wynona Rose, I specifically said products of BANTU
education. The moral of the story shall soon become evident.

Kgotsosfied Zoè I've never heard of these characters.

Xolani Ncame Never heard of the character.

Phathiswa Magopeni Tjo! I do not 'recognise' this question. *in that
parliamentary voice*

Mosekwa Tshikosi Std 1. My teacher had a huge stash of books that she let me borrow.

Thabani Madlala Ka-Afrika I was in high school in 93/94 and my younger sister went to a pre-school called Hansel and Gretel pre-what-what. Thought those were the names of the German couple who owned that establishment. Until I got into entertainment and started seeing the movies…

Phil Mhlongo I don't qualify I just wanna sit in this corner watch how this will end.

Fred Khumalo Thanks for your contributions. Okay, here's my long-winded summation. In 1985, my first year at tertiary, I made friends with some white dudes. Now, my new white friends were, like myself, very musical. So imagine their shock when they discovered that I didn't know who Bob Dylan was. Mama mia! I was initially embarrassed that I was coming across as a philistine. Then I had a lightbulb moment. I brought a Soul Brothers record to our commune. These white brothers did not know who the Soul Brothers were, at a time when this was the biggest crowd-pulling act in the country. It was my turn to express my shock! The lesson I learned was simple: because we were such a segregated country – even the airwaves were segregated (white radio, black radio) – it was quite possible to live in parallel universes where one side did not know what the other side was doing or learning. Sadly, this applied to education as well. Look, I have known about Hansel and Gretel for some time because these characters get referred to every now and then in great works of art. But it was only recently that I decided: you know, faark, just find the original book and discover what exactly this Hansel and Gretel story is all about. And I don't regret it. I have since discovered that in the white community it is a given that everyone is familiar with the tale. It's part of their pedagogical foundation. The responses that I got here indicate that those of us who were imbibers of Bantu Education were denied some of these foundational experiences. Another story that I read in my adult life is Alice in Wonderland. Through exercises such as this post, I have been able to ascertain, to some extent, that my ignorance of these childhood tales is not necessarily an isolated incident. But it's common among a certain age group of black South Africans. I hope that we will continue to break these walls, to destroy these racial laagers that deny a certain section of our community such a fundamental educational foundation.

Fred Khumalo And by the way, Vulindlela S. Kunene gave us an apt summary when he wrote: 'Fictional characters created from fables by famed Danish author, Hans Christian Erikssen [the Brothers Grimm are actually credited as the authors of the fairy tale]. My very model C primary school (am Swazi), brother and sister who got lost in the woods, brother's greed led to them eating a witch's house, witch caught them, wanted to spit-braai them, they escape, made witch pizza whilst doing so. The End.'

Vulindlela S. Kunene Glad for being misdirectedly helpful Ntungwa. I shall endeavour to read the instructions in great detail in future.

Isabella Morris Fascinating thread, Fred.

Coping with the
black-tax albatross

A few years ago, my sister-in-law introduced me to her friend, who, at twenty-five, had just finished her master's degree in psychology and was coming to me for help regarding her future career path.

'If you are looking for a job in the media,' I told her, 'I possibly could help you, but seeing that your focus is on marketing, I am stumped.'

She seemed shocked at these words. 'No, Bra Fred!' she said. 'I am not looking for a job. I was just wondering if I should perhaps go ahead and do my PhD, or if I should take the next year off, you know, so I can travel overseas and stuff.'

My armpits sweated; my ears itched; my lips trembled. A number of expletives rose to the tip of my tongue. What had this narcissistic nincompoop just said? This contumelious flibbertigibbet was surely poking fun at me! Her dilemma was whether she should do her PhD or travel overseas? And she was only twenty-five. And she was black.

Did she not know that at her age I was already four years into the world of employment? I wanted to tell her that at twenty-one, when I completed my journalism diploma, my parents did not have to remind me that it was now my responsibility, as the eldest of eight children, to find a job so I could put two of my siblings through varsity and the rest through school. There was no talk about honours degrees, or masters' and doctorates. It would only be much later, when I was already a father and a husband, that I would get my master's.

I know I speak for many black people when I say that our first salaries either had to go towards demolishing the shack our parents lived in so we could build them a proper house, or extending the existing government-issued four-roomed house into something bigger and more liveable. The permutation of our indebtedness to our immediate family differed from case to case, but it was there all the same.

If you didn't have siblings whose schooling needed to be paid for, then you had to pay the loan that your parents took out to put you through school. Or you had to repay the aunt or uncle who contributed towards your varsity education. That's black tax – it is unique to us. Of course, I'm not saying that all white people are trust-fund babies born with silver spoons in their mouths, and I know a few white guys who, after graduating from university, had to pay off their study loans. But that's usually about it. They don't have to fix their parents' shack, install electricity at home, settle their parents' medical bills, or even reimburse the neighbours who helped to subsidise their university education. Yes, in some villages, neighbours frequently decide that they want a graduate in the community, so they put their heads and wallets together to support so-and-so's child.

No one is celebrating this black-tax albatross. In the early twentieth century, when Afrikaners were emerging from English oppression, they too experienced familial burdens of this sort, which required that financial obligations be shared between parents and their children. To turn things around, they started cooperatives and building societies to stabilise families and build the community, one brick at a time. These micro-ventures, in turn, grew into formidable entities such as the Saambous, Santams, Sanlams and Nasperses of this world.

Thankfully, with each new generation the shackles of black tax are gradually falling off our figurative wrists as well – as they should.

I know that in my house, my children won't have to pay for each other's education. They won't have to fix my shack. The only black tax that they might have to cough up will be towards the Count Friedrich von Mntungwa whisky fund and miscellaneous contingencies.

City Press, **20 July 2015**

The rotund fence-jumper

You must never ever judge a book by its cover. This lesson, which I learned a long time ago, again came to mind as I listened to the testimony in the trial of Major General Bethuel Mondli Zuma, the man who would have been Gauteng commissioner of police by now had his previous criminal record not been exposed.

The scene of his crime was Alexandra Road in Pietermaritzburg, on 19 December 2008. Senior provincial traffic inspector Karen Bishop and her fellow officers had been conducting a roving alcohol roadblock at the scene when a white Mercedes Vito sped past them, failing to stop after being flagged down.

Bishop and her colleague, Kerwin Johansen, got into their patrol car and, with sirens blaring and blue lights flashing, chased after the Mercedes for a few minutes, using a loudhailer to command the driver of the vehicle to pull over. At one point they lost sight of the car in a street in Pelham, but they soon spotted it parked outside a yard.

After ordering Zuma – who we are told is not related to the president – to get out of the car, the officers gave him a breathalyser test, which he failed dismally. He was three times over the legal limit.

Now here comes my favourite part: as Johansen was about to handcuff Zuma, the major general suddenly pushed him out of the way and ran towards a two-metre-high gate, over which he proceeded to leap. Looking at a picture of the stout man, you can imagine the acrobatics that these traffic cops must have witnessed. By this time every South African should be familiar with Khulubuse Zuma's girth. Now imagine a drunk man almost three quarters of that size, only slightly taller, and leaping over such a high gate.

I am not the only person to note how ridiculous this scene must have looked to an outsider. During his cross-examination of Bishop this week, Zuma's lawyer, Sergie Brimiah, asked her: 'Do you really expect this court to believe he [Zuma] can scale a two-metre gate?'

To which Bishop replied: 'Maybe he had an adrenalin rush' – a statement that was followed by hoots of laughter from court attendees.

On a more serious note, however, it is a tragedy that this incident, which took place in 2008, had escaped the knowledge of the authorities – to the point that national commissioner Riah Phiyega actually wound up appointing our rotund gate-jumper as a provincial commissioner, before having to withdraw the appointment when the embarrassing criminal charges pending against him were exposed.

While this particular aspect of Zuma's life was not discussed in court and has no bearing on his case, it's still something to keep in mind, seeing as this is not the first time that a figure of such dubious character has been given a position of authority in our police service. Take national commissioner Jackie Selebi, for example, as well as his successor, Bheki Cele. Given these disconcerting appointments, one would think that those advising the national commissioner would have been more circumspect about whom she invites into her office this time around.

Another intriguing element of this tale is that Zuma actually started his career as a bodyguard to Harry Gwala, the outspoken ANC Midlands chairman. He was later transferred to Shell House, the erstwhile headquarters of the ANC, where he protected Nelson Mandela, Walter Sisulu and, later, Thabo Mbeki.

In 1994 he participated in the Shell House massacre, in which ANC security shot dead nineteen IFP supporters who had tried to storm the ANC offices. Zuma appeared before the TRC in 1998 to seek amnesty for his part in the incident.

Police spokesman General Solomon Makgale told me Zuma joined the police force in 1995 when the SAPS – an amalgamation of the previous homeland forces, the previous SAP, and members of the liberation movements' armed wings – was launched.

Some of Zuma's comrades in the Pietermaritzburg structures of the ANC have already expressed their disappointment at his reckless behaviour during the drunken car chase. However, they are adamant in their belief that his appointment as provincial commissioner would have been the 'best reward' for him for the part he played in the struggle.

Therein lies the rub: I don't know if it's just me, but I think this tendency to appoint people to positions of authority based not on their skill, expertise, education and experience, but on the elastic concept of their previous commitment and contribution to the struggle is a faulty one. It's simply another case of 'We did not struggle to not be rewarded'. Is this what we want as a nation? And in this argument I am not limiting myself to the police service but to the entire edifice of government.

Of course, in any setting a new government will, and should, surround itself with people it can trust and who are loyal to the cause at hand, and can thus be counted upon to deliver on the agreed-upon mandate. However, I think inasmuch as political compatibility and common values should guide those in power in their selection of bureaucrats, so should the concepts of merit, suitability for the job, ethical behaviour and general probity – especially in sensitive and 'hard' areas such as policing, where we are clearly failing dismally as a nation.

In July 2013, Transparency International revealed in a survey that a staggering 83 per cent of South Africans believe the police are corrupt. In its Global Corruption Barometer of 2013, the organisation stated that South Africa was among thirty-six countries in which the police were seen as the most corrupt institution.[1] Just a cursory glance at the records of the country's top cops would seem to give credence to this belief. And if you have corrupt leaders, the cancer afflicting them is sure to infect the entire corpus.

Over the past five years we have been bombarded by scandal after scandal regarding police officials whose conduct and performance are antithetical to the respect for and implementation of law and order in the country: Jackie Selebi, Bheki Cele, Sbu Mpisane, Richard Mdluli and now Mondli Zuma. I think it's about time the policing fraternity looks more introspectively at the screening methods it uses before promoting men and women to positions of leadership. After all, they say a fish rots from the head.

Sunday World, 15 September 2013

Amazing Grace!

You gotta give it to Grace, the first lady of the kingdom just north. She has chutzpah by the bucket load. Doesn't give a damn what people think of her, or what she says in public. Just as long as it satisfies her ego.

What's the point of playing cosy-cosy with the masses when they do not have brains and balls enough to say, 'Enough is enough. The Mugabes' reign has to end now'?

Clearly these people deserve what they get. And Grace's audacity is what they will be getting more of now that she's thrown her glove into the ring, hell-bent on stepping into her husband's big shoes.

Speaking of shoes, it is no accident that when she donated hundreds of pairs of shoes to children in a village outside Harare in October 2015, every single pair was a size thirteen. The children's average age was five.

We know what happens on Friday the 13th. Nasty things. Those of us who believe that our fate is tied to the stars, take the threat posed by the number thirteen seriously. So when Grace Mugabe distributed those size-thirteen shoes to small children a few weeks ago, it wasn't some random act. It was calculated. It was symbolic of a larger concept.

Look at it this way: a shoe is not something you throw around haphazardly. In Middle Eastern culture, throwing a shoe at a person means you have reached the end of your tether. You are cursing them.

Also, do you remember the man who threw his shoes at George W. Bush at a press conference in Iraq back in 2008? Look what happened to Bush afterwards. And I wonder what happened to the man. I suppose the CIA has the answer.

So when Grace Mugabe decided to donate oversized shoes to children – especially in light of all the other things they are probably in need of – she seems to have been inspired by a notion besides mere generosity. Just imagine the conversation that occurred when she made her decision:

'Grace, the children are hungry!' her people said to her.

To which she retorted: 'Ag, dammit, Roberti *maan*, let's give them shoes!'

By choosing to distribute those shoes, she was clearly sending out a couple of very important messages.

Message number one: I am about to step into my husband's large shoes and you young people of Zimbabwe have to start feeling the discomfort that I am going to experience when I put on those shoes. The only way that will happen is if you put your feet into my own oversized footwear. And you better start getting uncomfortable now so that you can become accustomed to it. This way, by the time you grow up, discomfort will have become second nature to you and you will not bother me when I am ensconced on my throne.

Message number two: the walk to the future of Zimbabwe is going to be a long one. It will need shoes that are big and sturdy.

You should see the pictures of those children with their stunned faces holding the shoes. Some of the shoes are so large, they are about the size of a few of the children's heads. The photos of the incident, published in the Zimbabwean media, are really nasty. Some of the media's reactions to the incident are also noteworthy.

Political commentator Revesayi Mutede's observation of the entire situation had me laughing my head off. He claims Grace could not love her husband because, if she did, she would have helped him retire from public office so that he could finally have some rest. Mutede reminds his readers that in 2003 already, on the occasion of Mugabe's birthday and in response to a question in a

TV interview of where he saw himself in five years, Mugabe stated that he would be retired.

Mutede remarks: 'And here we are, 12 years later. He cannot even climb one single stair without several minders ready to fly like goal-keepers, in case he involuntarily makes for the ground. But the Bible says, "There is no rest for the wicked". So as the rest of decent-minded and cultured Zimbabweans pity the old man and wonder why they won't rest him, his wife and party urge him on. Don't stop, they say. Keep going up and down stairs. Keep on until you drop dead.'

I especially like it when Mutede likens Mugabe to a *skorokoro*: 'Mugabe is breaking down, but they push and push to restart him. Mugabe's wheels are punctured and his engine makes rattling sounds and puffs smoke into the air like it's on fire. He is overheated and needs to be taken off the road and parked permanently.'[1]

You got that part right. Permanent parking. But you are rushing things, Mutede. Let me lick the cobwebs of ignorance from your eyes, as we say in my neck of the woods. To start off with, what's love gotta do with it? Do you remember that song by Tina Turner?

The problem with romantics like you, Mutede, is that you take things a tad too seriously. You get so teary-eyed and soft-hearted that you do not realise that Empress Grace does not roll like that. Romance is not her cup of tea. She is a pragmatist, my dear Mutede. She's too big and ambitious to fill her little head with useless abstract notions such as love.

Are you like see-ree-yus, Mutede? *Love?* It's like all about strategy, darling. It's like Grace needs Robert in office while she's like consolidating her support on the ground, like.

With those shoes she distributed the other day, she's hit the ground running.

Sowetan, 7 November 2015

Musical reflections

'We have lost our language.'

That's the unsettling refrain that Jonas Gwangwa keeps throwing at me as we sit drinking tea and talking music, politics, history, philosophy, even fashion, at his house in Observatory, Johannesburg, on a fine Sunday afternoon in September 2012.

Spring is in the air; the trees are in bloom and the birds are chirping merrily, enjoying the respite from what has been one of the most ferocious winters in the city of gold. Why, just a few weeks ago, Johannesburg experienced snow, a rarity in this part of the country.

It's unfair that we should be holed up inside the house on a beautiful spring day while the sun is declaring its glory outside. But Gwangwa is still under the weather, recovering from a bout of flu.

At seventy-five, he is also not getting any younger. And it's as if in acknowledgement of his frailty and creeping mortality that he keeps talking about the legacy he and his peers should be leaving behind in South Africa. Or, more specifically, what will happen to the legacy that they will leave behind.

'We are talking past each other,' he says. 'We have lost our common language.'

Funny that he should be talking about the death of a common language considering he lives just a stone's throw away from the vibrant inner-city neighbourhood of Yeoville, a melting pot of cultures and languages. Here, you can consume *egusi* soup (a soup made with *egusi*, or melon, seeds) at a Nigerian establishment, share *sadza* (porridge) with a few Zimbabweans at yet another establishment, or debate politics with Lingala-speaking brothers from the DRC at Kin Malebo – which, once inside it, will give you the impression that you are in Kinshasa.

So despite being just across the street from all of this cultural richness, what is Jonas Gwangwa doing talking about the death of some common language when languages are so evidently very much alive?

'What I am saying,' he explains, 'is that on the face of it, we seem to be doing very well – with people learning each other's languages and culture; we are seemingly making progress at laying down foundations for a culturally diverse country and society. In this country, we now have *kwasa kwasa*, we have West African sounds, we have kwaito – so on the surface, we are a country that embraces everyone. But in the process of embracing everyone, we have alienated ourselves from ourselves. We are no longer sure who we are as South Africans. That's why I am saying we have lost our common South African language.'

When Gwangwa speaks about language, he is not talking about Zulu, Xhosa, Setswana or any of the other official South African languages. He is talking about the universal South African language – music. More specifically, the music style of *mbaqanga*.

'That sound was our universal South African language,' Gwangwa says of *mbaqanga*. 'But where is it now? Yes, one admits that a sound has to evolve, get touched by other influences and grow.'

Gwangwa argues that that is what happened to the blues – it got touched, it grew, evolved, and, like a great river, it developed some tributaries. So, from the blues we got jazz, we got bebop, we got rock 'n' roll, we got soul, R&B and, dare we say it, rap and all its varieties. American musicians, when they hit a cul-de-sac, know to always go back to the root of it all. And that root is the blues.

'We have lost the real root of South African music,' Gwangwa emphasises. 'That's why the kids coming up today are so lost musically, because they don't know the root, the source. We can't blame them. Record companies and promoters have failed to nurture this original sound. When you play it, you don't get invited to venues, you don't get recording deals – there's a sense that you are irrelevant.'

The journey

And so we go back to the source. It's a long journey with many twists and turns, as well as some surprising detours. Gwangwa's indignation at the death of what he calls 'the original urban sound' is justifiable when you realise that *mbaqanga* is the sound he was born into, musically speaking.

Mbaqanga, which originated at the turn of the twentieth century in South Africa's urban areas, is a hybrid style of music that took its lead from African interpretations of European missionary songs of worship and traditional African folk songs played in the style of American swing.

These were the days of such bands and combos as Gwigwi Mrwebi and the Harlem Swingsters, the Manhattan Brothers, Peter Rezant's Merry Blackbirds, the Boston Brothers, led by Sam Williams, and the Jazz Maniacs, featuring the legendary Zakes Nkosi on the saxophone. The names of the bands themselves are a nod to America's influence on the South African music scene.

'When one was growing up, there was never a shortage of venues where one could play, nor was there a shortage of reasons to play,' recalls Gwangwa. 'We played at people's weddings, beauty pageants, we played at social clubs, we toured and travelled the country to play at this or other venue for this or other reason.'

It is an undeniable fact that Jonas Gwangwa's first foray into the South African jazz scene, like those of many of his contemporaries, was predictably influenced by developments in American music. In 1953, a popular movie in the townships was *Young Man with a Horn*, featuring Kirk Douglas as Leon 'Bix' Beiderbecke, the talented cornet player. Many of Gwangwa's friends and contemporaries saw the movie and began having visions of themselves as the cool Kirk Douglas.

Hugh Masekela, Gwangwa's cousin and schoolmate at Trevor Huddleston's famous St Peter's College, recalls being sick with the flu when he was approached by the cleric, who wanted to know what he really wanted to do with his life when he grew up. Hugh, along with his friend, Stompie Manana – who would later become one of the country's top trumpeters – had been misbehaving so badly that their school grades were suffering. Sensing that the cleric was in a generous mood, Masekela said: 'Father, if you could get me a trumpet, I won't bother anybody anymore.' He still had *Young Man with a Horn* on his mind.

Shortly after that exchange, Masekela marched into the Polliacks Music store on Eloff Street in Johannesburg with a letter from Father Huddleston. He left the shop with a gleaming second-hand horn, using it afterwards in the lessons he received from a man called Uncle Sauda, the leader of the Johannesburg Native Municipal Brass Band. Masekela also honed his skills with Stompie's guidance. His friend, Knox Kaloate, had also become infected with the music bug and joined their lessons. Soon, more boys began participating. George Makhene put together a set of drums. Gwangwa got a trombone.

Gwangwa recalls: 'I originally wanted a clarinet as it looked good and was popular, but then I saw a picture of Glenn Miller with his instrument. I liked the fact that it was huge and different. So I settled for the trombone. I had no clue how it functioned. So I started experimenting with the sounds coming out of the instrument. Somebody had shown me what the B scale was, so by trial and error I started imitating other trombone players.'

The Trevor Huddleston Jazz Band became a hit, playing at a

number of venues in the larger Johannesburg area, and getting a lot of newspaper coverage in the process thanks to the reputation of Huddleston, who was a prominent anti-apartheid activist.

In 1955, following the implementation of the Bantu Education Act, African education was transferred from missionary control to the Native Affairs Department, which was headed by Hendrik Verwoerd. Rather than co-operate with the government, the Anglican Church decided to shut down St Peter's. The closure of the college also meant the collapse of the Trevor Huddleston Jazz Band, leaving the young musicians to scatter all across the country, with some abandoning their dreams of having a musical career forever.

But Gwangwa and Masekela soon found new avenues for their talents. In 1957 they were both offered places in the ambitious African Jazz and Variety, a revue in which entertainers covered popular songs of the time, such as Louis Armstrong's 'Blueberry Hill', sung by Ben 'Satch' Masinga; Harry Belafonte's 'Day-O!', covered by the Woodpeckers; and Bobby Bland's 'It's Gone and Started Raining', sung by Dolly Rathebe. The show had a successful national tour.

In late 1957, pianist and journalist Todd Matshikiza finished writing the music for *King Kong*, a musical narrating the life of the controversial boxer Ezekiel 'King Kong' Dlamini. Gwangwa and Masekela were required to copy the orchestral parts from the sketches which saxophonist Mackay Davashe and pianist Sol Klaaste were creating for the musical.

On 8 February 1959, *King Kong* opened at the Wits University Great Hall, which was the only integrated entertainment venue in Johannesburg. The musical had a successful run and toured South Africa's major cities, coming to an end in October that year. Not only were the musicians jobless again, but the apartheid dragnet continued to pull at them. They might have been free-spirited artists determined to explore as much of life, in all its complexities, as they could, but freedom was the antithesis of apartheid dogma, and they were to have many brushes with the law.

Soon after *King Kong* wrapped up its act, John Mehegan, a pianist and jazz professor from Columbia University and the Juilliard School of Music, carried out a few workshops for up-and-coming musicians such as Gwangwa, Masekela and saxophonist Kippie Moeketsi, and even featured them on two albums that he recorded for Gallo Records.

But the country's laws of segregation frustrated Mehegan's plans, and Gwangwa recalls how infuriated Mehegan was during a visit to Durban when he, hoping to play with a variety of local musicians, could not appear on stage with one of his favourites, Claude Shange, as apartheid laws forbade people of different races from performing together. So Mehegan devised a plan. During his performance at the Durban City Hall, he played his piano while white musicians played the drums and horns. But the audience could hear a bass accompaniment even though they couldn't see a bass player. In a statement highlighting the ridiculousness of the situation, as well as the laws which were governing it, Mehegan explained to the audience what was going on: 'Oh, yeah, by the way, our bassist is Claude Shange who is playing backstage because he happens to be black and therefore can't appear with us on stage.'

The incident caused a major controversy and was splashed across the newspapers. Needless to say, Mehegan was kicked out of the country by an embarrassed and angry government.

After the Mehegan encounter, Gwangwa, Masekela and Moeketsi joined Abdullah Ibrahim (then called Dollar Brand), who had formed a trio with Makhaya Ntshoko on drums and Johnny Gertze on bass. The result was a sextet called the Jazz Epistles. They played to full houses in Cape Town, specialising in bebop favourites from Dizzy Gillespie, Miles Davis and Charlie Parker, as well as evergreens from the likes of Duke Ellington and Fats Waller.

Again, Gwangwa's foray into Cape Town was not without its bizarre 'only in apartheid South Africa' moments. For example, after their performances in front of white audiences, they were not allowed to mingle with their fans and had to have their meals and drinks in the kitchen. Moeketsi used such infuriating experiences as inspiration for the band's humorously titled track 'The Scullery Department'.

During their Cape Town run, the band members stayed – illegally – in an apartment in Camps Bay, a posh strip of Cape Town where rich and famous whites lived. In order to remain at the flat without being kicked out, they had to enter it through a service entrance, masquerading as painters. The house painting had actually been completed, but the band left paint, rollers and brushes deliberately strewn around the apartment in case a nosy white neighbour ventured in to check that the darkies he'd seen moving in and out of the place were indeed painters. The band made sure to always come home long after midnight, to avoid being spotted by any inquisitive eyes.

In 1960, the Jazz Epistles travelled to Johannesburg, where they had a successful run, culminating in the recording of their album, *The Jazz Epistles Verse 1*. The band was so tight that they recorded the album in two hours flat.

Conquering America

After the closure of St Peter's, Father Huddleston returned to Britain, but he kept in touch with some of his protégés in South Africa, especially Masekela, who kept pestering him for a scholarship. Eventually, in 1960, Masekela received the nod to go to England to study music. Meanwhile Gwangwa got his opportunity to leave the country when *King Kong* toured the United Kingdom. When the musical finished its run in London, Gwangwa stayed on, regularly hanging out with his friend and cousin Masekela.

Soon, however, both musicians found the London scene rather stultifying. They were determined to go to the birthplace of jazz, the United States, and by 1962, they were sharing a flat in Manhattan, New York, and studying music at the Manhattan School of Music.

'The music was good – we brushed shoulders with the likes of Freddie Hubbard, Miles, Dizzy – but life was rough. We survived on Campbell's soup and bread. In fact, our supplies of the soup were sometimes so limited that we had to supplement it with water. That's the life of an artist, that's the life of an exile.'

Speaking of exiles, it was around this time that Gwangwa and Masekela started opening their flat up to newly arrived South African students, including Willie Kgositsile, and many others who were jazz aficionados, artists and scholars in their respective fields. 'Even though I was soaking up the American jazz experience, I did not want to lose my accent, musically speaking,' says Gwangwa.

Gwangwa was working hard, and established musical voices such as Harry Belafonte, who had his own music publishing company, were noticing his efforts. When Belafonte went to the studio with Miriam Makeba for their unforgettable *An Evening with Belafonte and Makeba*, the American utilised Gwangwa's expertise as a producer. The album was Makeba's sixth in the six years since she had left South Africa, and would go on to win her a Grammy Award in February 1965.

Gwangwa in the meantime was shuttling all over the United States, living in various cities and states, including Boston, Rhode Island, Atlanta and California. He and Masekela, as well as their homeboy Caiphus Semenya, would stay with each other every now and then, but like typical exiles with no fixed abode, they kept moving.

Exile can take a toll on you. Nowhere is this better captured than in an anecdote that Masekela provides in his autobiography, *Still Grazing*: 'I would often go to Central Park across the street from

our new flat, find a solitary area, and talk to myself in all the different home languages I could muster.' He was soon mistaken for
a lunatic, and a policeman was called to the scene to take care
of him.[1]

On another occasion, he and Gwangwa felt so homesick that,
together with some of the exiled students, they decided to do the
unthinkable. Having caught wind of a rumour that you could find
goats in some of New York's ghettoes, they went looking until they
found one. The trick then was how to get a goat into an apartment
in snooty New York City. No problem. They dressed it up in a coat
and a cap and, travelling in a taxi at night, managed to sneak it into
the apartment, where they proceeded to slaughter it in a tub. Such
was the life of an exile.

The team of Gwangwa, Semenya and Masekela continued to
write songs for artists such as Miriam Makeba and Letta Mbulu
(Semenya's wife, who arrived in the US in 1965). Masekela had also
recently married Makeba. In 1966, Gwangwa featured on Masekela's
album, *Grrrrr!* Shortly thereafter, Gwangwa hit the big time again
when his composition, 'I Wanna Go Home Now' (performed by
Mbulu and her band, the Safaris), entered the top-100 singles charts
in both *Cashbox* and *Billboard* magazines, the industry's bibles.

After the collapse of his marriage to Makeba in 1966, Masekela
found himself shuttling between Los Angeles and San Francisco to
perform with his band Oo-Bwana. He had also started a record label,
Chisa Records, which had recorded the Crusaders. The Crusaders
would later accompany and record with Mbulu, on material penned
by Gwangwa, Semenya and Masekela. So taken was the trumpeter
Herb Alpert with the new sound of Gwangwa and Masekela that
he collaborated with them on the famed national tour, The Main
Event, in 1967.

For this, 'Herb was reviled by some jazz purists for his open-
mindedness and his experimentation,' says Gwangwa. To him and

Masekela, however, it 'was refreshing to work with him as we had time and space to "speak" fluently in our own indigenous *mbaqanga* tongue'.

Gwangwa and Masekela had clearly heeded Miles Davis's advice when he told them, after listening to their music, to play their own South African shit. There were thousands of great American jazz trumpeters with whom Masekela would have had to compete if he had decided to go the American route, and if he had, he might have ended up just being a statistic. But sticking to their roots allowed Masekela and Gwangwa to procure the attention of many music followers who were entranced and intrigued by this rare sound.

Towards the end of the 1960s, Gwangwa moved from New York to Los Angeles, where he stayed with Semenya. Masekela was in San Francisco, but when he heard that Gwangwa was in the City of Angels, he quickly moved there himself, forming a new band with his old-time friends called the Union of South Africa. They immediately embarked on an intense rehearsal schedule, culminating in an eponymous studio album, *Union of South Africa*.

Gwangwa was overjoyed with the result: the sound of the album was home-brewed *mbaqanga*, with Gwangwa and Masekela playing all the solos, and Semenya on the saxophone and singing improvisations. Gwangwa's piece, 'Shebeen', a traditional Xhosa folksong groove, was the highlight of the album. The rhythm section was comprised of members of the Crusaders: Wayne Henderson, the group's trombonist, played drums; their saxophonist, Wilton Felder, played bass; Joe Sample was on the piano; and Arthur Adams was on the guitar.

In his book, *In Township Tonight!*, David Coplan writes about the sounds of the Union of South Africa: 'Masekela, Gwangwa, Semenya, and others showed doubters wrong by proving indisputably that South Africa's own marabi-rooted jazz tradition was worth developing and expanding and playing. Their live celebrations of Africa's modern musical spirit in the United States were an unforgettable experience.'[2]

The Union toured the US extensively. They later relocated from the West Coast to use New York as their base. On the East Coast, they hooked up with the poet Amiri Baraka (formerly known as LeRoi Jones), who helped put together a tour for them, which would be headlined by Miriam Makeba.

That's when fate struck: a day before the tour kicked off, Gwangwa was hit by a car and badly injured. He wouldn't be able to perform for months. However, as the showbiz adage goes, the show must go on, and the band toured without him, hitting cities such as Philadelphia, Washington D.C. and Pittsburgh. But Masekela admits: 'Without Jonas, our efforts paled against [Makeba's] sizzling performances.' The group broke up, and the members returned to Los Angeles. In an attempt to replace Gwangwa, the group decided to go to London, where a few South African musicians were based. They hooked up with saxophonist Dudu Pukwana and drummer Makhaya Ntshoko. The result was *Home Is Where the Music Is*, based mainly on Semenya's instrumental compositions.

When Gwangwa was released from the hospital, the Union of South Africa tried to make another album. But it was not to be. It became clear during rehearsals that there just wasn't any chemistry there anymore, so they abandoned the project. And that was the end of the Union.

Homecoming

In 1978, Gwangwa was in the studio again with Alpert and Masekela to record their album, simply titled *Herb Alpert & Hugh Masekela*. But by the 1980s, many exiles had started trickling back to Africa, closer to home. Gwangwa was one of them. In 1984, a major festival of the arts called Culture and Resistance was held in Botswana, attracting hundreds of musicians, writers, painters and artists from various disciplines. Old friends such as Dorothy Masuka, Barney Rachabane and Kingforce Silgee reunited there.

After the festival, Gwangwa decided to stay on in Botswana. In 1985, he narrowly escaped death when members of a South African death squad bombarded his home as well as those belonging to several other ANC exiles.

Gwangwa then had to leave Botswana for Tanzania. Shortly after that he was recruited by the ANC to start an a cappella music group that would help channel the energies of restless youngsters at the ANC camps, some of which had experienced mutinies. The result was the Amandla Cultural Ensemble, an energetic vocal and dance group that would capture the imagination of many in the years to come. The activist in Gwangwa was now given free rein to use music as he'd always wanted to: as a weapon of struggle.

In 1987, Gwangwa collaborated with George Fenton to compose the score for *Cry Freedom*, the Richard Attenborough–directed film starring a young Denzel Washington as Steve Biko. In addition to being nominated for Oscar, Grammy and Golden Globe awards, the film score received Ivor Bovello and Black Emmy awards.

When Gwangwa came back to South Africa in 1991 he was shocked and disheartened at how uninterested the country's music establishment was in his music and that of his fellow travellers, Masekela and Semenya. 'When we asked for performances from promoters, we were simply told that our sound was no longer relevant,' he says.

Since returning to South Africa, Gwangwa has spread his wings into other areas. He wrote the signature music for the popular soapie *Generations*, and also released numerous albums and documentaries. The *mbaqanga* jazz sound is at the percussively throbbing heart of his music. It is what the blues is to American popular music. Gwangwa continues to emphasise why it is so important:

This is the root, the source. How can it be irrelevant? However, with the passage of time, I began to get it: of course if you want to frustrate a people's creativity, you shut the source. And that's exactly what happened. They realised that with this sound we could say potent things, that the sound was too powerful. So they sought to undermine it and alienate it, as they did with the original blues in America. But thankfully, American musicians are resilient; they protected that sound by all means necessary – that's why new young musicians are still able to go back to the source, whenever they hit a cul-de-sac in their artistic expression.

Gwangwa argues that even though we might have an ANC government, the producers of culture remain part of the old establishment, and they don't want intellectually liberated masses. He decries the fact that the government has not done much to sustain the artistic endeavours that helped advance the cause of the liberation movements while they were still in exile. He argues that artistic expression played a major role in spreading the message of freedom in the darkest days of South Africa. It was only on 16 July 1963, when Miriam Makeba famously addressed the United Nations Special Committee Against Apartheid, that the international community began to realise the horrors of apartheid, experiencing it through the eyes of a female musician who had hitherto maintained a largely apolitical stance, and whose music had mostly appealed to a black audience.[3] Later, the work of the Amandla ensemble intensified the anti-apartheid message to the international community through its performances, which spanned a period of ten years.

But now that the ogre of apartheid is dead and gone, the potency of the arts as an agent of social change is no longer appreciated. 'It's neo-colonialism in the cultural world. Unfortunately black people with the power and means to intervene are complicit to this suppression of our tongue. We triumphed over those Americans because we refused to be them; we played our shit, as Miles said. But now, we are trying our damnedest to be them.'

And we are failing dismally at it, because, ultimately, the American language is alien to us. We might mimic the twang, but we don't have the tongue.

'We have lost our language,' insists Gwangwa.

The fine and terrible line that apartheid collaborators walked

Jacob Dlamini has written a messy book. It is a book that could, on impulse, make you want to dissociate yourself from it because it has you feeling complicit in what it seems to be advocating: namely, an all-out witch hunt for apartheid-era spies and collaborators.

Except that *Askari: A Story of Collaboration and Betrayal in the Anti-Apartheid Struggle* sends out no such clarion call. It's complex. It problematises the problematics, seeking refuge in academic lexicon.

The book is ostensibly about Glory Sedibe, a top-ranking member of the ANC and its military wing, Umkhonto we Sizwe. In August 1986, Sedibe, codenamed Comrade September, was abducted from his hideout in Swaziland by members of an apartheid death squad led by the notorious Eugene de Kock. Spirited back into South Africa, Sedibe was then interrogated and viciously tortured over a period of one year.

It is not long before Sedibe starts telling his captors about his comrades in the ANC. Not only that: former intelligence operative Barry Gilder, who was interviewed for the book, constantly reminds us that, as time went by, Sedibe became even more enthusiastic in pursuing his former comrades, even, apparently, when he had not been prompted by his new bosses to do so.

This suggests that Sedibe had made a moral choice to not only betray his MK comrades, but to actively participate in hunting down and annihilating the same soldiers who had trusted him with their lives.

Throughout his analysis of Sedibe's actions, Dlamini – who holds a PhD from Yale University – refuses to accept easy answers. No one is let off the hook. In fact, at the percussively throbbing heart of *Askari*, Dlamini excoriates all South Africans who were alive at this time, claiming that every one of us was a collaborator, to some degree, within the apartheid behemoth. Even now, in post-apartheid South Africa, it is clear that the evils of the system still have their tentacles in every walk of life. Each one of us has been touched by it, whether we like it or not.

I have already mentioned the massive amount of discomfort that the book inflicts on its reader. Once you have subjected yourself to the last sentence of *Askari*, you might find yourself slowly dropping it to the floor, before taking a deep breath and leaning back, as if to physically distance yourself from the horrors you have just been exposed to.

On another level, a sense of relief might also follow you once you are done with the book – relief from the knowledge that a brave and visionary soul has taken the time to create an outlet through which others will be able to deal with the issue of collaboration. I found that simply plunging into this sordid tale of betrayal – whether the book goes on to reveal that the betrayal was witting or unwitting – was an exercise in self-catharsis. As I moved through the narrative, I kept pausing and asking myself: when I did what I did, did I do enough, and was it the right thing? Why did I behave in that manner, as opposed to the other way? Whatever the case, the manner in which I acted was unforgivable!

Reading *Askari* a second time, if you are brave enough to do so, will only feel like a form of self-immolation, because you still won't be able to find any easy answers to these questions. By writing about our history in this riveting and ruthless manner, Dlamini has some-how found a means of becoming everyone's confessor. The Truth and Reconciliation Commission might have been conceived as the balm to the wounds sustained by South Africans and our national body politic, but this book is the scalpel that seeks to reopen these wounds. And while it will hurt, looking again at how these wounds were formed, as well as at the pain that they caused, could give us another chance to remove any impurities that still remain within them.

Furthermore, if the TRC was a platform on which we could give our confessions (sometimes half-heartedly) and ask for forgiveness – thus allowing us to rush for our hymn books and sing the doh-ray-me-fah-sohs of reconciliation – Dlamini's book is the discordant, strident voice that stops us and says: hold your *simunye* horses, friends, we have a lot of unfinished business. Answer my question: why did you do what you did?

In my own history, this question pertains most to my experiences as a young man in high school, where I was appointed a prefect in standard nine because of my good academic scores and the commitment to order and discipline that I frequently demonstrated. This was in the 1980s, when the lines between the establishment and the masses were clearly defined and being a prefect was risky business. It could lead to one being branded a collaborator, which was usually a sweeping epithet reserved for functionaries of the repressive system of apartheid, such as teachers, policemen, councillors, public servants and even shopkeepers. As we all know, the price of being a collaborator was a dire one which usually included death as its final, and most decisive, form of punishment.

For my own part, I could easily have turned down my appointment. However, my belief in order and discipline superseded all other considerations; it blinded me to the dangers of having a foot in the 'wrong' camp.

I never had sleepless nights about the situation, either, as I still saw myself as part of the masses. After all, I would share with my fellow students the same banned or 'undesirable' literature – from the likes of Steve Biko, before he became fashionable, as well as Jomo Kenyatta, Marcus Garvey and Chinua Achebe, among others – and I was called on numerous occasions to lead a few *umrabulo* sessions (*umrabulo* were informal political education discussions which were common in the townships in the 1980s).

During break time, I was one of the 'merchants' selling cigarettes in the toilets. I even turned a blind eye to the dagga smokers and the knife carriers. I walked the same dangerous streets with the latter and I understood that, in many cases, those knives were not for show.

But even with all those things in mind, I would still not allow any of these fellows to be late for school, to make noise in class, or to be disruptive. Not on my watch. I was required by school regulations to compile the names of wrongdoers, and that is what I did. That is all. There were certain times, however, when I, like Glory Sedibe, would go the extra mile and threaten wrongdoers with physical violence. What is more, being a prefect had exposed me to hidden dangers which I had never considered when I accepted the appointment. At any point during this period, the security police, who were ubiquitous in schools, could have approached me (possibly through the guidance of a teacher, for example) with questions on who among my charges were the perennial troublemakers, the usual suspects.

And yet 'troublemakers' was a loaded word, not least because it was never clear to us students what exactly made someone a troublemaker. A person who asked too many questions at school could be labelled a troublemaker; but so could someone suspected of having relations with well-known political activists who were in exile or jail. What was clear was that being branded a troublemaker was definitely a punishment most people did not want to endure, and, indeed, some pupils my age were detained without trial for being suspected as such. Thankfully, it never came to pass that I was asked to point them out. But it certainly could have happened. And what would have stopped me from doing so?

In the years that followed, a close friend of mine, Vusi Maduna, who had also led *umrabulo* sessions at his school and was a trusted activist in his community, was rumoured to be an apartheid collaborator.

Even though we were from opposing political camps – he was a Charterist and I was a Black Consciousness adherent – we had been pretty close at one stage. When we finished school, he became a teacher and chairman of the Hammarsdale Youth Congress, an affiliate of the UDF, while I became a journalist.

When the rumours started circulating that he was a spy I naturally avoided him like the plague. Then, in 1987, while visiting Clermont, he was killed by a group of UDF comrades. And he was forgotten, just like that.

It would only be during TRC hearings in May 2000 that his name would crop up again. One Jabulani Wiseman Mzimela applied for amnesty for Maduna's murder. During the hearing, it was revealed that the rumour that Maduna was a spy had started when he was seen talking to some white people in the township. Mzimela pointed out that Maduna had recently had his hair permed, which indicated that he had lots of money, and many people began wondering where he got it from.

Mzimela had never seen Maduna before the day he killed him, but he confessed that he was satisfied with the explanations from UDF comrades who lived in Maduna's neighbourhood that he had money because he worked for 'the system'.

Personally, I will never know for sure if Maduna had indeed been a spy. But, after reading *Askari*, I couldn't help remembering his story or asking myself if I'd been complicit in any way in the murder. As a journalist, I had the power and the means at my disposal to investigate or even confront him on the rumours, especially given our past relationship. Does the fact that I did none of these things imply that I was afraid – if it turned out that Maduna was a spy – that he would turn on me? Or that I would turn on him?

And if he was a spy, what were his reasons for becoming one? I don't remember hearing anything about him being detained and tortured. Clearly the lines of fault and blame that circumscribe this affair are much more complex and blurred than they appear to be on the surface.

Still, while my own possible guilt in what became the accepted history of Maduna's life is technically non-existent in the eyes of the law, it underlines how problematic it is to continue framing apartheid wrongs merely in the form of the perpetrator-versus-victim narrative – a process which the TRC adopted, and which Dlamini takes issue with. In such a context, while Sedibe has been portrayed by some as a victim who had no choice but to be an agent or be killed by his captors, Dlamini candidly states that the man made a choice not only to deceive those he had a moral obligation to protect, but to actively, and voluntarily, go out of his way to participate in their pursuit, torture and, possibly, murder.

Dlamini then moves on from this argument to present us with the story of Mark Behr, a former Stellenbosch University student who would later become a famous novelist and literary scholar. As a student, Behr spied on fellow students on behalf of the apartheid security apparatus.

Behr's case provides yet another kind of extreme to measure on the collaborator–victim scale. In this instance, the difficulty exists in determining his motives for spying. It seems that while some people, like Sedibe, became askaris and enemy agents on pain of death, others did so simply because they were seduced by the idea of being so close to power. In his confession to the TRC in July 1996, Behr says that he spied for the apartheid state because they paid for his studies. What is more, he thinks that the lack of malice and ill-intent he displayed even while collaborating means that his actions deserve less judgement than, say, those of a collaborator who was motivated by more insidious intentions: 'while I have not murdered or tortured, and while it is unlikely that my activities on a campus like Stellenbosch led directly to any such atrocities, I must and do take responsibility for my contribution to making "the system" work. There cannot be, and will not be any justification for this.'[1]

The problem is that not once in this self-serving and rather smug confession does Behr actually tell us what he did. Nor does he indicate to whom it was done, or when, or how. But by including Behr's story in his narrative, Dlamini is making the point that there are no black and white areas on the issue of collaboration; in fact, he seems to indicate that there are too many grey areas. He goes on to argue that collaboration should rather be looked at as a continuum, with some forms easily considered more heinous or evil, or as having a greater impact, than others. But I take issue with the simple glossing over of the problem offered in this instance. Looked at from this point of view, at what point do you draw the line? When do you decide that one act of collaboration is more or less evil than another?

Consider Behr's case again. If acts of collaboration can really be accepted as having taken place within a continuum, does this mean that Behr's sins are less severe than those of Sedibe's? It is difficult to pass that judgement because, in the end, we do not know if his actions resulted in the destruction, whether literal or philosophical, of others' lives.

*

In the 1990s, when I was a young journalist for *UmAfrika*, a left-leaning, Catholic-owned weekly, there was a strong rumour circulating in struggle circles that ANC Youth League leader Peter Mokaba, who was also a member of the ANC underground in the

Northern Transvaal, was an apartheid spy. But no one was prepared to tell this story. This was Mokaba, after all. A very big fish. It took one Gavin Evans, a progressive journalist from the *Weekly Mail*, to publish the truth about Mokaba in *Leadership* magazine in 1994. His story was a sensational one.

Dlamini provides further details of how the ANC came to find out about Mokaba's activities. Having heard a claim by a student that Mokaba had attempted to recruit him as a spy for the security police, as well as one by an activist who said Mokaba had set him up to be intercepted by the police, Mokaba was detained in one of the ANC's prisons in Zambia. Through interrogation he eventually confessed. However, Oliver Tambo was hesitant about keeping Mokaba in detention, and he did not want Mokaba's confession publicised, believing that this would cause disillusionment among the youth fighting in the struggle. So Mokaba was allowed to return to South Africa, free but under certain conditions.

In the politics of resistance fighting, Mokaba had come full circle. He had been tortured by the state, who then directed him to spy on his comrades. When they found out about his betrayal they spared his life, getting him, in turn, to deceive the apartheid state that had been paying him a few pieces of silver in exchange for information. But whether the intelligence he gave to his handlers led to the death of any of his comrades is not the issue Dlamini chooses to focus on. Instead, he shifts his gaze to the choices made by the major players in the situation: by Mokaba and by Tambo, who chose to look the other way when confronted with the truth of his comrade's treachery. Again, messy stuff. It brings to mind a question Antjie Krog posed about the extent to which the decisions of desperate and suffering people can be judged: 'What are the invisible links between being tortured into breaking your own moral codes and later corruption, between giving up everything in the fight for freedom and eventual greed?'[2]

Considered in this context, should it surprise us, then, that many of yesterday's liberators – with their previously high, unassailable moral codes – have become today's looters, betraying the very dream that they fought so hard to achieve? Or is this simply the way humanity rolls?

Maybe it is more accurate to realise that we as South Africans have been putting too much premium on values instead of accepting the fact that human nature evolves, and that with that evolution comes changed priorities and idiosyncrasies.

A proximity to the feeding trough would indeed change the order of things, as well as the way you view it: eat now, amass as much as you can and at whatever cost, all while appeasing the masses with occasional scraps of platitudes and nuggets of wisdom about values and moral regeneration.

A nagging question remains, though. Specifically, who has actually betrayed whom? Have the leaders betrayed the people who trusted them to lay a foundation for an ethics-based, value-driven society? Or have the people collaborated in their own betrayal by placing too much trust in a leadership corps that was tortured and stripped of their self-worth – a leadership corps which, at the first available opportunity, behaved like their former oppressors, visiting the same torture, albeit in a new, more nuanced guise, on those they were supposed to defend and protect?

This argument is mine, not Dlamini's. And perhaps this is too cynical a view to take on South Africa as a nation right now.

Whatever the case, Dlamini is bold in his declaration that the current establishment is awash with people who were functionaries of the old regime. Eugene de Kock, who spoke freely to Dlamini about Sedibe and other askaris, confidently points out that had Sedibe lived (he died in 1994 of heart failure, or poisoning, depending on who you listen to), he would have been occupying a top position in government today.

By complicating how we think about apartheid and its many and varied legacies, Jacob Dlamini has done well at challenging South Africans to scrutinise the disavowals at the core of our collective memories – even if this means sacrificing what we have always believed about others, or ourselves.

Having read the book, and considered it in the context of my own experiences, I get a sense – not for the first time, I'm afraid – that without properly examining these memories, South Africans will continue to move, like somnambulists, into a dark, uncertain future.

Rand Daily Mail **Online, 6 November 2014**

The Trump factor

I was highly offended when I found out that Donald Trump has been depicted as a pile of faeces in a giant mural in Lower Manhattan. The mural, the brainchild of American graffiti artist Hanksy – well known for his pun-filled stencils and parody paintings which regularly feature movie star Tom Hanks as their subject – gained notoriety soon after Trump announced he was running for president.

I am offended because I believe Hanksy is being unfair towards a pile of faeces. A pile of faeces, at least, has some positive use. You can turn it into manure, for one thing. And as a seasoned gardener, I can tell you that manure from human waste will produce bigger and healthier vegetables than a garden treated with regular fertiliser.

Faeces is also useful in that it provides flies with nourishment and homes for dung beetles. In other words, piles of faeces are crucial in maintaining a balance in the natural ecosystem.

By comparison, Trump does not balance anything. Instead, he tends to disrupt everything. He insults black people, threatens Mexicans, declares war on Muslims, says nasty things about women, pokes fun at disabled people and brags constantly about his riches.

He is clearly far worse than a pile of faeces. A pile of faeces would probably blush in embarrassment at the mere comparison to such a man. I know that 'Trump' rhymes with 'dump', but this does not give us the liberty to reduce a pile of faeces to Trump's position.

Consider it another way: the act of producing a batch of waste comes, for the most part, from a gentle and natural process that provides a lot of relief to its maker – sometimes pure joy, in fact.

There's nothing joyous about Trump. Take some time and look at his face. Even before he opens his mouth, you can't help but be startled by the perpetual scowl on the man's countenance. It's an expression that is indicative of a strange strain of retardation which psychologists are yet to attribute a name to. It is the scowl of someone who is highly constipated yet refuses to seek succour in the toilet. It is the scowl of a man with a cricket bat stuck up his behind.

Given this unfair and very uncalled-for incident of faeces-shaming, it therefore came as a relief to me when someone else, in a rather smart move, used Photoshop to have a picture of Trump's face appear on the wall to which a real-life lip-shaped urinal is attached. While not a true depiction of the urinal itself, the Photoshopped image, which makes it seem as if the urinal is Trump's mouth, certainly is a funny one – although I wouldn't want to use such a thing to relieve myself if it did exist, no sir. I wouldn't want Trump's lips – even a two-dimensional copy of them – near or around my you-know-what, ever. I have far too much respect for my private parts to even consider exposing them to Trump.

So when Trump blow-up dolls started appearing online for sale, I was naturally quite disturbed and disgusted. Yurgh! Defiling your imagination and your body on a likeness of Trump the dump? Definitely not *ayoba*.

When Donald Trump toilet paper and 3D-printed Trump butt plugs started selling, however, I finally felt like they were on to something. For some reason, using toilet paper with Trump's face on it to wipe your behind seems to me more repulsive than a real pile of faeces. I don't know why, but that's just the way it is.

And then there is Portland artist Sarah Levy, who has painted Trump using a menstrual-blood-covered tampon and paintbrush.

This after Trump's public insinuation that a female news anchor who gave him a hard time was menstruating. To me, that does the job as well.

But regardless of which creation is the most disgusting or remarkable, they all form part of a fascinating trend, this outpouring of art attacking the image of Trump. Judging by the number of artworks using controversial or taboo images (or sometimes actual bodily excretions) to portray him, it could be deduced that there is something off-putting, or even repulsive, about the man's appearance or demeanour. Something that makes people think of waste and filth. He certainly makes me think of the devil's halitosis, and I don't even know what that smells like. But the stench must be worse than anything imaginable.

The man really seems to embody the worst American characteristics: he is crass, arrogant and bigoted. And like Adolf Hitler, who blamed Jews for the problems of post–World War I Germany, Trump is blaming American problems on foreigners, mainly Mexicans and Muslims. He has already said that if he becomes president, he will kick Mexicans out of the US and then build a massive wall on the border between the two countries to prevent future in-flows of refugees. Not only that, he says, but Mexico will also be required to finance this wall.

He has a big thing coming his way, however, if he thinks he will actually succeed in any of these ventures. Deporting all of the US's Mexican immigrants – a people who are so deeply ingrained within America's DNA – would require tons of effort, especially since the majority of them probably don't want to leave.

The same goes for Trump's declaration that he will ensure all Muslims are barred from entering the US. Does he not know that America has millions of Muslims who were born and bred there? This includes figures such as Muhammad Ali, Louis Farrakhan, jazz pianist McCoy Tyner, jazz musician Ahmad Jamal, and many others who are less famous.

It is all very unsettling. A lunatic of his stripe sitting in the White House will only mean hell for the rest of the world. How many wars is he going to declare if he actually succeeds at winning the presidency?

Even more worrying for me, though, is what a potential President Trump says about the American people themselves. I would have thought that after the warmongering Bush family, the whole nation would be more circumspect about who they put on a pedestal of power. It is the string of events that followed Operation Desert Storm – as the first foray into Iraq was called – which contributed to the War on Terror, the effects of which the entire world still continues to deal with today. In varying degrees, we have all been touched by the events Bush senior instigated back in 1991, only to have his son complicate the fallout even further, and all in the name of establishing democracy in the Middle East.

Now, Donald Trump? Lord have mercy!

Sowetan, 11 December 2015

Boom boom boom!
Malema bites the dust!

And there I was thinking my Malema was our new commander-in-chief. But he gets floored by a security guard – a simple *mantshinge-lane*? I've lost faith in this cowntri. The last time I saw a leader letting down his people like this was when Eugène Terre'Blanche allowed himself to be thrown off a horse!

Facebook, 25 November 2014

Tommy Ntsewa And Sam Shilowa too – signs that the end of an era is nigh – Mene teke...

Zolani Nkosana Felix Kuku Don't underestimate the power of the machengelane. Remember the one that dropped the guy in front of The Spear?

Sibusiso Zondi All that goes up, will come down – gravity...

Respect Deejay Vernon Hehehehe.....did the Mantshingelani have a baton at least? Hahahah.

Fred Khumalo My heart goes out to the young man. He's been eating too much cabbage from his cabbage patch. The effort of releasing all that flatulence has left him very weak.

Dr-Skhosiphi Mvikeleni Cele He got some radical physical engagement from one of the people he claims to be representing.

Thabo Masemola Amasolokohlo – kwathi gumbuqe kwathi mbo. Zakhehla komdala (kwasho iGxaba lembadada). [That's how he met his demise. So said Gxaba Lembadada.]

Thula Butheezi Mbulazi you have to go back to the Sunday Times Baba. We miss your pieces.

ShottaZee Nchema Rapoo In his defence, it had just rained and the floor was declared slippery.

Zipho Shusha Waze wangibulala ngensini weMntungwa. [You are killing me with laughter, Mntungwa.]

Melanie Askeland Oh dear, your heroes have feet of something like clay.

Majid Jarboui The Terreblanche one is amazing, looooool.

Trevor Mfeka Uhlekisa umuntu ecashile [You make a person laugh out loud, even from a hiding place], do you remember how Mbazima Shilowa fell from a horse?

Harri Narismulu Any idea on the colour and the state of ventilation of JuJu's brief. Maybe Jani can do a comparision???

Meza Ceza Haa haa haa.

Pule Monnaruri What if it was you? Would you expect sympathy or mockery? How are [you] building anything by scoffing?

Carol Fagan Ha, ha the bigger they are........... If only this charismatic person could channel his ego more and employ more logic, he could be a force to be reckoned with. In all fairness he has challenged some pertinent issues, albeit in a self-indulgent way. He needs a proper spindoctor!!!

Patricia Manshon Well said!

Phil Mhlongo The horse was black LOL.

Sithembiso Malusi Mahlaba Salute to 'march on the line' well done!

More Jujus, tea girls
and cowboys needed

We have powerful characters in this country, and thankfully we do not hesitate to tell them what we think of them, usually in colourful language.

We have a president who no longer bats an eyelid when we call him the Kangaman, or Showerhead. The man has taken all these barbs in his immeasurable stride – so much so that he seems to be immune to all other attacks lobbed at him of whatever kind.

Have you noticed how he has turned the Nkandla imbroglio on its head? Now, it's as if his detractors are the ones who need their heads read. What a character.

Then we have his deputy, Cyril Ramaphosa, known as McCyril the Killer thanks to a popular T-shirt that features those words and the head of a buffalo – a reference, perhaps, to the buffalo which he bid nearly R20 million for at an auction some years ago, drawing the ire of Julius Malema and others.

There is also Mmusi 'Broken Nation, Broken Man' Maimane, who is beginning to sound like a broken record now. Can he go home and rehearse another memorable speech, or is he a one-hit wonder?

Pity the National Tea Girl, Lindiwe Mazibuko, who is plying her trade at Harvard. And yes, she finished her master's, graduating in May 2015. Congratulations. We've always known that wasn't sawdust between your ears.

Like Maimane, Jujuboy is sounding like a broken record now,

too. #Paybackthemoney, #Paybackthemoney. Come on, fat cheeks, you can do better than that. We need to be distracted from Nkandla and all other woes. It is becoming too depressing.

Also, where is Bheki 'Stomach In, Chest Out' Cele? Some call him the Cowboy Sugardaddy. Come back, baba, let's drive the fear of God into the hearts of the criminals. Shoot to kill. Just as long as you don't shoot yourself in the foot.

And what about the pipe-smoking intellectual? A little bird tells me he was seen with the Kangaman Nkandlaman the other day and said to him: 'Jacob, don't you think it's time you said goodbye to the people of South Africa?' To which the president responded: 'I must say goodbye to them? Where are they going?'

At Eskom, they can't keep the lights on long enough for them to finish counting the millions they are going to give the new-but-about-to-be-fired CEO as his golden handshake.

They hire a national director of public prosecutions, but the minute he starts doing his job they say: 'No, comrade, the digging wasn't part of the deal. Here's your golden handshake. Go.'

With the mounds of creativity we South Africans have, I wouldn't be surprised if there is already a private club hidden somewhere in our suburbs where former CEOs of our parastatals sit and compare notes: 'Okay, Motsoeneng, how did you manage to fool them for so long? Can you give me your *inyanga*'s cell number? He must be dispensing some real powerful muthi.'

'Comrade Nxasana, what they gave you makes Dali's handshake look like small potatoes. Explain?'

'Ag, comrade, it's simple: just tell them you have tapes that show them playing with mermaids in that fire pool and they'll let you go with a handshake that's super golden. Hahaha!'

And yet, even in the face of all this drama, we South Africans can at least find consolation in the fact that we have a constitution and a bill of rights that are still worth the paper they are written on. We can still laugh at our freedom, thanks to these documents. Not so elsewhere in the world.

Look at Zambian musician Chama Fumba, who was arrested on 8 June 2015 after he performed a song about a character named Lungu who has no ideas but carries a suitcase full of bottles of whisky. Lungu supposedly refers to Zambian president Edgar Lungu. The song has taken parts of the Zambian nation by storm.

For his alleged mockery of his president, Fumba faces a penalty of up to six months in prison or a fine if he is convicted, although his attorney is pleading the artist's right to freedom of expression in his defence. His arrest recalls an incident in Zimbabwe when a man was jailed for tearing down a poster featuring the face of President Robert Mugabe and taking it to the toilet, where he was going to put it to good use.

So I am glad that people in this country continue to test the limits of freedom of expression, whether it be through controversial paintings such as *The Spear*, which was displayed at the Goodman Gallery in 2012, or *maskanda* musician Phuzekhemisi singing in protest against a poll tax imposed by local chiefs on people who own dogs.

It is only proper that we – the small people who do not have fire pools in our backyards – keep trying to cross these boundaries. If we do not, the powers-that-be will not hesitate to start eroding, and then uprooting, each of the entrenched freedoms that we enjoy. And it is only with these liberties that we will find any succour during the days when we are just the playthings for those in power.

Sowetan, 13 June 2015

Speaker? Parliament needs a security guard

Had I not spent inordinate amounts of time inside a classroom staring at a teacher performing her magic on the blackboard, I probably would have been a taxi driver or a security guard.

That's because in KwaZulu-Natal, where I am from, these are the two professions that come easily to those who do not waste their days sitting at a desk. And in my neck of the woods, where we are stubborn and predisposed to order, such qualities will stand you in good stead for these occupations.

I can hear you sniggering as you consider the connection between taxi drivers and order.

Yes, taxi drivers are actually very orderly. Otherwise, how do you explain the fact that they uniformly succeed in refusing to pay tax? Apart from footballers, I can't think of any other professionals who love forming themselves into clubs and associations the way taxi drivers do. That is a sure sign that you are committed to structure and discipline. The problem in the taxi business, however, is that each and every chairman of an association believes his version of order cannot be questioned. If you do question it, he will use his hands to nudge you into his own line of thinking.

For outsiders – always eager for easy answers – this might be misconstrued as violence or 'taxi wars', but all taxi drivers are trying to do is to get people to see things from their perspective. As this can be somewhat difficult to achieve, taxi drivers have to keep trying and trying.

I don't know how long it will take for fellow South Africans to understand that the laws that govern them do not apply to taxi drivers.

The taxi drivers themselves keep trying to drive this point home. They have their own set of laws, and only they are privy to them. So perhaps it's best that you leave them alone now, since they obviously know what they are doing.

It also helps, as I mentioned earlier, that the pursuit for order in the taxi industry is accompanied by a generous supply of stubbornness. If you are not stubborn, it's difficult to succeed at maintaining discipline.

When God was dishing out qualities to human beings, he certainly blessed KwaZulu-Natal with deep, bottomless reservoirs of stubbornness. Security guards, who are the cousins of taxi drivers, stand as the epitome of the province's characteristic pig-headedness. It is therefore no coincidence that the most successful security guards come from KwaZulu-Natal. Like taxi drivers, they are committed to bringing people under their command. And similar to their taxi-driving counterparts, they are known to use their hands to do so – which has created the unfortunate impression that they, too, are violent.

Which brings me to the Zulu word for security guards – *omantshingelane*. The genesis of this word is amazing, dating back to the second half of the nineteenth century when trains were first introduced into what was then called Natal. One of the main considerations for a successful railway service is security. It makes sense, then, that as soon as the authorities decided to start rolling out the railway, the first thing they did was to set up a corps of security guards.

Security guards, however, do not grow on trees; they are trained. And while scouting for would-be security guards, it was in my part of the world that the authorities discovered an abundance of potential.

After recruiting these would-be trainees, the company gave them uniforms and began drilling them. The men were taught to march in line and their instructor would inspect them every morning as they stood there. Then he would bellow, 'Okay, march in line, march in line!', and they would dutifully obey him.

When it was time for them to graduate and their friends and wives wanted to know what exactly it was that they were going to be doing for a living, one of the graduates, unable to properly pronounce the order he was given every day to 'march in line', produced a warbled version of the phrase, then walked up and down to make sure he was getting his point across.

When the wife was asked by her friends what her husband did, she said: 'My husband *umantshingelane*' – repeating what had come out of his mouth when he had tried to say 'march in line'.

Clearly Julius Malema is not aware of this history of South African security guards, which is why he clashed with one at Emoyeni Conference Centre in Johannesburg in November 2014.

When the security guard tried to search him, Malema refused, so the guard had to push him back in line. Unfortunately, he was a wee bit enthusiastic in his efforts and Malema ended up falling as a result.

A friend who witnessed the physical interaction between Malema and the guard said the latter later apologised for his actions: '*Cha, asilwi. Siyakuqondisa nje.*' (No, we are not fighting. We're just straightening you up.)

Perhaps Parliament should consider hiring a security guard as speaker of the house to restore order there. I think it would work wonders.

Rand Daily Mail **Online, 28 November 2014**

What is a national key point?

Is Sizakele MaKhumalo Zuma's spaza shop at the Great Palace of Nkandla a national key point?

What about the presidential fire pool? Are the mermaids who have been spotted swimming in it with Khulubuse themselves national key points? Is the cattle culvert at the palace one as well?

These and other related questions are about to be answered.

I first heard of national key points back in 1985 when I took a press law course as part of my journalism studies. One of the cases we tackled was that of a British tourist in South Africa who was arrested for taking a picture of a section of the harbour in Durban.

Kicking and screaming, she was dragged to court, where it was explained to her that she had contravened the National Key Points Act by taking that picture. By doing so, she had endangered the security of the state.

Soon after this, the subject of national key points began dominating dinner-table conversations. Everyone wanted to know what exactly a national key point was.

Luckily for me, my journalism textbook was a tome called *The Newspaperman's Guide to the Law*, which, among other things, dealt in great detail with this question. Four or five pages dedicated to this subject left me and my class in no doubt that no one knew what exactly a national key point was.

But maybe I'm exaggerating.

A national key point could be a police station, a harbour or any government 'installation', according to the National Key Points Act of 1980. You were not supposed to approach a key point if you had no reason to. You were not supposed to take a picture of it, either.

In my journalism class, we wanted to ask questions about all of this but we were discouraged from doing so. See, asking questions in South Africa in those days was considered to be highly impertinent. Baleka Mbete would probably have felt right at home there. She strangles questions before they are even born.

Like many South Africans who had read about the arrest of the British tourist, I stupidly assumed that this piece of legislation would not be allowed to rear its head in a democratic state. So imagine my shock when I found out that photographing sections of the Nkandla palace was in contravention of the illustrious National Key Points Act.

Younger journalists assumed it was a new piece of legislation, causing veterans such as myself to smile proudly at our superior knowledge. No, we told the youngsters, the National Key Points Act dates back to apartheid days. But they chose not to believe us and googled the darn thing. Google ultimately vindicated us.

Impressed by the superior knowledge of their older mentors, the youngsters then wanted to know what exactly a national key point was. That was when we delivered the real blow.

Well, we said, a national key point, you see, is a location that becomes a national 'key' point based on the opinion of whoever is in power.

In current-day South Africa, the National Key Points Act is a real boon. It is a wonderful piece of legislation because it covers a lot of ground without bothering with specifics. And who needs specifics anyway?

We are not like those rude kids from the EFF who want to ask a specific person to pay back the money specifically used for improvements to a specific abode that may or may not be a key point. No, we don't deal in specifics. We are contented South Africans who use our votes wisely every five years.

I think it is only proper that this piece of legislation was pulled out from the vaults of apartheid-era laws and put to good use again. It seems a suitable weapon to protect us against our enemies. Some unpatriotic people might be suggesting that this legislation was only invoked to distract the media's attention from the Great Palace of Nkandla, but this is obviously not the case, especially since the government will soon be shedding some light on the entire area.

On 3 December 2014, the Johannesburg High Court ordered minister of police Nkosinathi Nhleko to hand over the list of national key points and national key point complexes within thirty days to the Right2Know Campaign and the South African History Archive.[1] The minister had originally refused to release the list's contents, claiming that such a revelation might put the country's defence and security at risk.

Personally, I think it's important that all South Africans know where the national key points are so we can stay away from them.

It will also be interesting to discover the status of the Great Palace of Nkandla in relation to the act since all the reports I have read on this matter are contradictory. While one report, tabled by public works minister Thulas Nxesi in 2010, states that the palace is, in its entirety, a national key point, others suggest that only certain parts of the palace are national key points. I would like to know if MaKhumalo's spaza shop is one.

If it is, it will be a great pity, because then we won't be able to approach it – even if we want to support MaKhumalo and be true to the spirit of BEE.

With BEEated breath we wait.

Rand Daily Mail **Online, 5 December 2014**

Zuma: I want my
day in court ... Not

It was one of those surreal moments when the viewer has to do a double take and wipe his eyes so as to focus properly on the scene unfolding on the television. The man on the screen was in full throttle, almost in tears, as he told the nation: 'All the buildings and every room we use in that residence was built by ourselves as a family and not by government.'

Forever the cynic, I thought I was maybe watching Pieter-Dirk Uys in blackface doing a Jacob Zuma skit. But no, it was the president of my country in person, taking questions from members of Parliament about the ever-ballooning cost of his Nkandla compound. That was November 2012. I had not seen the beginning of his address, hence my disbelief when I heard him tell the nation that the compound had been built from the Msholozi clan's private coffers.

I would later watch a re-run of the address and be shocked, once again, at the country's Citizen Number One fibbing with such eloquence; he would have shamed Uys, David Kau and other professional actors and comedians.

Even when Zuma made the statement, there was already mounting evidence contradicting him on some of the minutiae in the growing saga. For example, during the address, he professed that his family had obtained a bond from FNB for the upgrade to his residence. A clear lie, as banks do not extend home loans for structures built on communal land, and Nkandla is situated on land owned by King Zwelithini's Ingonyama Trust. But that's just one minor aspect of all the inconsistencies central to the Nkandla saga.

Public protector Thuli Madonsela's report on the swindle – which at first had the very appropriate provisional title of 'Opulence on a Grand Scale' – helps to put the entire shebang into proper context. Now we get a thorough breakdown of how R246 million was spent on the compound.

Admittedly, it is only proper that the president's abode be given a proper security upgrade befitting his office. As a functioning democracy in which the principle of the separation of powers reigns supreme, it is justifiable that the executive enjoy its autonomy and the privileges and responsibilities that come with the territory. As our president once famously proclaimed when he was questioned about the reasoning behind the e-toll system, this is, after all, not Malawi.

But what is shocking regarding the cost of the Nkandla compound is that, following a police security assessment carried out in May 2009, the public works department had initially estimated the Nkandla upgrade to be around R27 million. How this ballooned, in a matter of just over three years, to R246 million defies comprehension and logic.

Adding to concerns that there must be something malodorous surrounding both the security upgrade and the enhancements made to the compound – many of which seem to be rather esoteric; consider the spaza shop and the R1-million kraal – are how determined Zuma and his current minister of public works, Thulas Nxesi, have been in trying to prevent Madonsela from making her findings public. Why all the secrecy? Why the insults hurled at Madonsela for simply doing her job?

It is only thanks to her steadfastness and her commitment to airing the matter in public that we at least know a bit more about

Nkandla. Undoubtedly, though, what we think we know might just be the tip of the iceberg.

One detail that has surfaced concerns an incident that occurred in August 2009 – just months after the security assessment had been conducted – when Zuma decided he wanted to have a hands-on approach in the construction of Nkandla. Others would call this political interference.

During this time, Zuma demanded that three new houses be built on the compound, which necessitated further security enhancements. He then had his private architect, Minenhle Makhanya, introduced to the department of public works, after which he became the principal agent for the upgrade.

Madonsela's report tells us that Makhanya is a schizophrenic of some sort. As the department's agent, he was supposed to ensure legitimate security enhancements were done cost-effectively. But wearing his other hat as the president's private architect, he found himself bowing to Zuma's demands and tastes before any other duties or obligations he might have had. Madonsela has a nice expression for this kind of schizophrenia: conflict of interest.

Schizophrenic as he might have seemed, Makhanya and his bank manager were nevertheless fortunate to not experience any headaches from his duties as his fees were calculated as a percentage of project spend. As the costs ballooned, so did his bill.

Madonsela enumerates other enhancements which she describes as excessive and unlawful, and which should not have been part of a security upgrade. Included among these are a visitors' centre costing R6.7 million; a cattle kraal estimated at R1.2 million; and the relocation of some of the presidents' relatives at a cost of R7.9 million.

The report contains many more details about Nkandla, all of which raise more questions than answers. Having perused it, I doubt anyone beseeching the president to take the nation into his confidence and respond in detail to the report's enquiries will feel unjustified in their demands. And there's no better platform to do this than Parliament itself, where he can give his explanations to his ANC comrades and other parties.

There is no better time than now, Mr President, to clear the air and help us understand just what happened, and exactly how it happened.

I do not doubt that he will do this. Our president is known for his sense of humility and co-operation. On a number of occasions now he has called for his day in court. Even though each time this is about to happen, a few gremlins crop up that tend to derail the entire process.

Maybe this time around we can hope that the president will finally indulge us and jump with alacrity at the opportunity to address us on this issue, which, like the arms deal, seems to be distracting him from doing his job of governing the country.

Sunday World, **18 August 2014**

In March 2016, the Constitutional Court found that President Jacob Zuma failed to uphold, defend and respect the Constitution in the matter of Nkandla and ordered that he pay back an amount deemed reasonable by National Treasury. In June, Treasury set the amount at R7.8-million.

Khulubuse: grow up
so you can reign

Four people were injured, one of them seriously, when a section of the disused Aurora gold mine collapsed on them. Contrary to earlier reports, the collapse at this once-controversial mine in Springs was not occasioned by the activities of illegal miners – the so-called zama-zamas – but, according to underground sources, by former owner Khulubuse Zuma.

Zuma, who also happens to be President Jacob Zuma's nephew, recently paid a secret visit to his former stomping ground to see just how much more things have degenerated since his departure.

A security guard, who accompanied Zuma during his tour of the mine, said things were going well for most of the visit. At one point, Zuma even shed a tear at the sight of the dilapidated buildings and rusty and ruined machinery. When a worker from Mr Delivery arrived with Zuma's lunch, which contained a family meal from Nando's – a chicken complete with a salad, six rolls and a two-litre Coke – the guard believed the visit would continue as it was once Zuma had finished his meal.

But Zuma, whose stomach had greeted the appearance of the meal with a loud growl, merely looked at the food with a confused expression before turning back to the delivery man. 'What do you take me for?' he exploded. 'I said somebody must get me lunch! Nando's people all over the country know what Khulubuse's lunch is! And you come here with a snack! You just want me to lose my temper so that the newspapers will hear about another Zuma being in trouble!'

To everyone's surprise, Zuma began to cry. 'Everybody hates the Zumas! I order lunch, and they send me something that I can fit into one of my nostrils and still be able to breathe without difficulty. And when I complain openly about this injustice, I will be told that I am full of self-entitlement.'

Throughout his outburst, Zuma had been stomping the ground with his feet – and that is when it happened. After several crashing thumps, the ground caved in, and Khulubuse went down with it.

Thanks to his quick reflexes, the security guard managed to jump to safety. The chap from Mr Delivery, however, was not so lucky. He fell down the hole and was buried under the food he had brought for Khulubuse.

The fast-thinking security guard then called for emergency help. Paramedics who arrived at the scene took one look at Khulubuse's face protruding from the hole and knew that they were in for a lot of work.

They decided to call on the help of a nearby farmer, who provided a span of twelve oxen from his farm in order to pull Khulubuse from the rubble. A harness was tied around Khulubuse's upper torso as well as under his armpits, and the oxen, bowing under the crack of the farmer's whip, sprang into action.

They pulled and they pulled and they pulled, but their attempts were fruitless. Khulubuse was stuck, and now he was in pain as well, as the harness was eating into his flesh. Eight of the oxen would end up dying in the attempt.

This is when somebody suggested that the Waterkloof Air Force Base intervene in the matter. But Khulubuse immediately disputed the idea. 'No, no,' he cried. 'The last time my uncle had dealings with that Waterkloof outfit, the family name got dragged in the mud. I can't afford to be associated with Waterkloof at all.'

His head suddenly turned. A few metres away, some security guards were gathered around a box of *iskobho* (sheep's head), which they were gulping down with pap and atchar.

'What about me?' Khulubuse shouted. 'I want *iskobho*, too!'

The security guards ignored him and continued eating. But the incident had given one of the rescue personnel an idea, and soon a helicopter was flying over the mine with a whole side of lamb tied to a rope and dangling above the hole where Khulubuse was stuck.

The earth started to shake as Khulubuse, trying to get his hands on the meat, attempted to lift himself off the ground. But his efforts, which included a fierce round of jumping, helped to break away at the rubble that covered him, and he quickly found himself free from his trap. A steel ladder was unfurled from the helicopter and Khulubuse grabbed on to it with both hands.

As the helicopter took off, listing to and fro from the immensity of Khulubuse's weight, it seemed for a moment as if it would crash into the ground. Fortunately the pilot was a professional, and he was able to ground the helicopter safely on a landing strip a good distance away from the sunken mine. The minute the helicopter came to a stop, Khulubuse, still coughing from the dust he had inhaled inside the hole, began to eat the lamb he had gripped onto throughout his journey.

As Khulubuse ate, he started speaking, half to himself, half to the security guards who had accompanied him from the mine. In a forlorn voice he said, 'We can't choose our parents, we can't. Take me for example. Zulu boy born in KwaMashu of poor parents. But poor as they were, they were also ambitious. Perhaps overly ambitious. Otherwise, why would they give their poor child such a name? Khulubuse! Do you know what Khulubuse means?'

The guards, both of whom were from Zimbabwe, shook their heads hesitantly. While they knew that Khulubuse was a Zulu name, they were not familiar with its meaning, which is actually quite poetic. Khulubuse is a contraction of 'khula', meaning 'grow up', and 'ubuse', which means 'so you can reign/feast'. Khulubuse, therefore, is a positive appellation that can be defined as 'grow up so you can reign, or feast'.

Khulubuse burped, and then laughed when he made this revelation. He probably felt proud that he was part of a deeper narrative that exposed the hopes and ambitions his parents had had for him. There are times when the name of a child tells the story of a family at the moment of his birth, or of the land into which he was born. Undoubtedly, Khulubuse's parents – destitute and downtrodden as they were – could see in their new baby the future man who would redeem their family name. A man who would grow up to reign, and feast.

The guards listened respectfully as Khulubuse told them his story. He had shown so much pride in the origins of his name that they were surprised at the sudden change of tone in his voice as he said: 'Gentlemen, can someone phone that rude fake Zulu Fred Khumalo and tell him to put me in contact with his friend, Somizi Mhlongo? I'm sure Mhlongo will be able to help me deal with this weight problem of mine. It's become so bad that the Guptas have stopped inviting me to their house. This can't go on. My time to reign and feast can't end like this.'

Then he fell asleep.

Pirates need some potent *korobela*!

Dear Sis Dolly,

It has been quite a while since I've written to you about my abusive spouse Pirates. This is because I thought he had mended his ways. How he dealt with that harlot from across the road, Lazy Thiefs, in October 2015 convinced me that he had turned over a new leaf.

In the early years of our marriage he was never prepared to indulge the Jezebels of this world who would distract him from his course. His commitment was solely to our happiness together. Oh, how I enjoyed those days! We were truly the Happy People. I would find myself swelling like a vetkoek made of self-raising flour at all of his achievements. We were kicking arse, my spouse and I.

That wily *magosha* from Pretoria who goes by the name of SkyIsTheLimit was kicked in the butt as well. Just because she comes from a rich family she thinks she can throw her weight around! Rhha! *Aneva!* My man Pirates was not confused or impressed by Sky's riches. He kicked her in the butt and moved on. He was a real man. Always bringing home the bacon.

Sis Dolly, in all honesty now, can you blame me for having rested on my laurels? I thought I had every reason to sit back comfortably on my throne with the full knowledge that my spouse was so committed to my happiness, he was like the throbbing of my own heart. 'What's my name, little harlots?' I said, as Thiefs and Sky licked their wounds.

But, alas, my moment of celebration was short-lived. I learned my lesson: never be complacent if you are in an abusive relationship. Keep your eyes open. Stay on your toes. Always have one hand on your man's shoulder. Make sure to guide him so he doesn't lose direction again. There are many temptations and pitfalls in this world and, as we all know, men have the attention span of an EFF member of Parliament.

So with all this in mind, I am coming to you, Sis Dolly, to report that my man has had a relapse. The other night he fell for the charms of a damsel from some backwater called the Free State. I can't even find this place on the map. Is it called the Free State because the harlots over there give it away for free?

The particular harlot who bamboozled my man is named Stars. That's another travesty: that a streetwise man like my spouse could fall for the charms of a tikkieline from the back of beyond – a thing with the temerity to call herself Stars. If her name had been Beatrice, Elizabeth, or even Beyoncé, I might have understood. But Stars? Clearly my man is losing his touch, wouldn't you say, Sis Dolly?

What makes everything worse is that the *magosha* from across the road, the one we call Thief from Phefeni, is having a field day. In fact, she didn't even sleep last night, celebrating my bad fortune. She drank *ngudu* after *ngudu* of Castle Milk Stout Chocolate mixed with Smirnoff to give it a kick. That's how unclassy she is. Sies!

Sis Dolly, I am prepared to suffer nearly all indignities, but to be laughed at by that toothless, one-breasted, cross-eyed road crosser called Hazy Thiefs? No, Sis Dolly, not on my couch.

And please don't try to remind me about the other night when my spouse dealt so effectively with that harlot from the small coal town in the east. What's her name again? Oh yes: Aces.

Yes, he was able to sort out that lass from Witbank. But, Sis Dolly, such an unpredictable, errant performance does not do much to inspire more confidence in him. We are still in trouble and I cannot start celebrating just yet.

I know you are going to say that I am behaving like an ungrateful snivelling beawtch, Sis Dolly. But, hey, cut this girl some slack. Once bitten, twice shy. I need my spouse to regain his form and kick butt consistently before I can relax. In the long run, it is better to operate from a base of pessimism than to perch yourself on a pedestal of positivity and be knocked down by some beawtch you would never even have looked at twice before. I have been disappointed too many times, Sis Dolly.

Now, Sis Dolly, some time ago, when the abuse at the hands of my spouse was at its worst, you gave me a concoction, a *korobela* which proved highly potent and efficacious. I put only a few drops of it in my spouse's drink and he became a raging bull. We were Happy People again. After having of the *korobela*, he simply kicked out of the way every obstacle that showed up in front of him with a venomous commitment. I think it's time for that kind of intervention again. I need that *korobela*, ousie. At my age I can't keep up with the abuse I keep getting from Pirates, let alone the heart attack that seems imminent if it continues.

Yours in tears,
Dudu from Orlando

***Sowetan*, 26 February 2016**

The day Brilliant went missing

I am one of those emotionally fragile characters who will cry when the sun nudges the morning landscape with its warm fingers, or when a rainbow bruises the sky.

I cry when a child is born, or when an unwitting foot tramples a poor ant to death, my beautiful black face left drenched in tears. When I sink my teeth into a succulent piece of steak and my taste buds stand up and cheer, tears fall onto the meat like drops of Worcester sauce. Beauty and cruelty trigger the same response in me – tears.

This weekend I cried when Pirates played Chiefs, for reasons that shall soon become clear. But I cried even more a few days later when, on Tuesday 10 November 2015, a week before Bafana Bafana's campaign against Angola, the news broke that Brilliant Khuzwayo, the Chiefs goalkeeper, would not be joining the national side.

I cry easily.

I cried because having Khuzwayo on the squad – his first foray into international football – would have been good for the young man. It would also have been wonderful for the team. But above all, I wept because, as a Pirates man, I felt personally responsible for Khuzwayo not joining the squad.

I cry easily.

The official story that has been given to the media about Khuzwayo not playing in the national team cites family commitments as the reason, but this is nonsense.

I'll tell you why Khuzwayo is not in Angola. I am actually surprised that the gods of football journalism have not yet woken up to this story. Perhaps my editor will notice this and look on me kindly when it is time to hand out bonuses at Christmas. If you think about it, I am breaking a story that even eluded the likes of hotshot journalists such as Bareng-Batho Kortjaas.

Admittedly, I only stumbled on the truth when I, being the conscientious journalist that I am, decided to interview Khuzwayo after the match on Saturday. But before I could get to him, those beefy Chiefs security guards elbowed me out of his way. Undeterred, I traced Khuzwayo to his place the next day.

It was while I stood in front of his house waiting for a chance to speak to him that I spotted the ambulance. Ducking behind some cars, the better to keep an eye out for developments, I watched as Khuzwayo, lying on a stretcher, was loaded onto the emergency vehicle. No sooner had the stretcher disgorged the young man into the back then the ambulance sounded its siren and began driving away at high speed.

But that was not the most interesting thing I witnessed outside Khuzwayo's house. Guess who was watching over the entire proceeding? None other than staff nurse Doctor Khumalo himself! Yes, the one who used to play for Bafana and who is now doing I-don't-know-what-exactly for the Kaizer Chiefs technical team.

I followed the ambulance all the way to Chris Hani Baragwanath Hospital, where I spent the whole of Sunday trying to smuggle myself into the ward where Khuzwayo was being kept. But every time I got inside the reception area, my tears would get in the way whenever a curvaceous nurse passed me by.

Upon seeing a man in a Chiefs T-shirt being rolled into reception in a wheelchair, his head covered in bloody gashes – is this how Kaizer Chiefs fans celebrate? – I broke into a fresh round of tears.

Before long, a security guard came up to me and accused me of freaking out the patients. A hospital is no place for tears, he told me sternly. But as I tried to leave the reception area, another security guard grabbed me and began pushing me into the inner recesses of the hospital.

When we got to the psychiatric ward, he said to me, 'This is where you belong.' Then he handcuffed me by one of my wrists to a bedframe, declaring triumphantly as he left, 'People who cry for no reason belong here!'

'But I'm not mad!' I protested to his receding figure. 'I am a journalist!'

A man lying on a bed nearby laughed when I said this. He attempted to console me: 'Welcome home, brother. When I got here I thought I was not mad. I thought I was Jomo Sono!'

I spent the rest of Sunday in that position. When I screamed, they would Taser me. It was only on Monday when a nurse, who is an old flame of a friend, recognised me and came to speak with me.

Having listened to my story of how I came to be there, she said, 'But, Fred, I've always said you are a madman in denial. I will let you go home today, but you need help. Anyway, you know who I've just seen?' She looked around to make sure no one else was listening. 'Brilliant Khuzwayo!'

'Serious?' I said.

'See-ree-yus! I'll take you to the ward.'

When we got there, Khuzwayo was sitting on a bed. Both his arms were encased in plaster of Paris.

What a scoop! But I couldn't help myself, and I soon began crying again when I remembered how poor Khuzwayo had sustained those injuries to his arms.

Those heavy volleys and shots from Pirates on Saturday were no child's play.

Sowetan, 13 November 2015

Cure this man of his gout, or else ...

Gout is a vicious ailment. The only comforting thing about this big sickness with a small name is that it is not contagious. Otherwise, I would have contracted it a long time ago, what with the number of veteran sufferers of the disease who I know.

What I am about to say is based on observation only as I have no clue what the onset of gout actually feels like. You will therefore have to grant me some poetic licence in this case. It seems I'm tempting fate just by writing about it, however. When I mentioned my intention to do so, a friend who has been in and out of the gout trenches said to me, 'You speak about that thing' – he won't mention it by name lest it reveal itself there and then – 'it's sure to get you, my friend.'

His warning reminded me of my childhood, when we were told not to speak about lightning while there was a storm in progress: 'You want this house to be struck by lightning?' was the reason that was given to us to remain silent.

I have poked endless fun at gout sufferers while being very grateful that the ogre has not yet wrapped its tentacles around my own limbs. But I'd also like to explore (and possibly explode) a few myths surrounding this ailment. Some years ago I worked with a chap who could be seen almost every other week hobbling into the office in his sandals, proceeding at a pace that would have made the common garden snail look like Usain Bolt. Every time I saw him in that state, sweating like Julius Malema after an encounter with

SARS, I would take off my imaginary hat and salute gout. People who thought they knew everything about it would smile knowingly and opine: 'Too much red wine and brandy.'

But the guy was a born-again Christian and a teetotaller, which seems to indicate that gout gives the humble grape a bad name. I've been worshipping Bacchus for many years and I have never been struck down by the illness. My carnivorous diet happens to be legendary as well, yet I have not once been at gout's mercy. All of this assists in blowing up myth number two: that meat consumption makes one susceptible to gout.

On to myth number three. For a long time gout was portrayed as a very sexist ailment that only attacked men. But this is untrue. I have two female friends who genuflect at the feet of this conqueror.

You see, no one can be sure what exactly causes gout. Some of my friends are medicos, and one of them happens to be a sufferer who can wax lyrical about the medical reasons for the illness when he is not in the grip of it. Something about uric acid deposits becoming concentrated around your joints if you eat rich foods, etc. I never listen to him because history shows I'm impervious to catching this little disease. But I also don't hear him out because, if what the doctor was saying were true, he wouldn't be suffering from it as he does now. He would have known how to relieve his symptoms.

And yet, for me, this lack of a cure for gout has had a more uplifting side to it, too, because if you approach a friend at the exact moment that he is in the clutches of this agony, he will oblige you with anything, as long as you bloody well leave him alone.

You want his car keys? 'Take them!' Want his wallet? 'Take the bloody thing and disappear!' he'll scream. Wanna kiss his girlfriend? Okay, you are pushing your luck now.

But you get my drift. A person suffering from gout is dangerous because he is not in control of his faculties. He cannot be trusted with a car, a gun or a cup of hot coffee because he can use one of these at any point as an outlet for his agony.

He can plough the car into the nearest ditch, or empty the magazine of his gun into his own leg, or pour hot coffee over his skin – anything that promises temporary respite from the pain in his feet.

This is why I got very worried when I heard that Kim Jong-un, the North Korean dictator, has gone underground, and the rumours are that he has gout.

Dictators are, by nature, a dangerously unpredictable species. Add gout to the mix and you have an apocalypse. Mr Kim is not your typical playground dictator, either. He is a dictator with gout *and* a nuclear bomb.

This is the same chap who had his uncle, Jang Song-thaek, executed for committing 'tremendous crimes against government' in December 2013.[1] Only someone in the throes of gout could dream up such flamboyant charges. I wonder what accusations he will throw at the world as he, sweating and groaning in agony, reaches for that nuclear-bomb button.

When the likes of the Supreme Leader of North Korea gets attacked by gout, I think it's time to start taking matters seriously and plead to the medical fraternity to find a permanent cure for this thing.

Rand Daily Mail **Online, 17 October 2014**

For the meek shall inherit the earth, amen

On my first visit to Nigeria a few years ago, I stumbled upon a church called the Holy Ghost on Fire Ministries. This was in Abuja, the Nigerian capital.

Then I saw another one, also in the capital, named Guided Missiles Church. I suddenly found myself developing an interest in the churches, not because I was seized by a need for spiritual sustenance, but because I was astounded by the sheer number of them. There was a church on almost every corner.

This multiplicity of churches was even more pronounced in Lagos. Every third building in the city contained a church of some sort.

The old joke goes that in Nigeria, you stand on a street corner, pick a stone, throw it at random and you are likely to hit the head of a professor – because in Nigeria, everyone is educated.

Here is my new take: stand on a street corner in Lagos, pick a stone, throw it at random and you are likely to hit the head of a church pastor – because in Nigeria, everyone and their dog is a pastor.

Religion is big business in that country. The third-richest pastor in Nigeria is Prophet T.B. Joshua, whose net worth ranges somewhere between the paltry sums of $10 million and $15 million (about R157 million to R235 million, as of May 2016), based on a Forbes list of richest Nigerian pastors.

The richest pastor in Nigeria is Bishop David Oyedepo, who

is worth $150 million (about R2.35 billion) according to the same list.

Oyedepo owns four private jets, a publishing company, a university and a high school. His church has space to seat 50 000 people, which means monetary possibilities are limitless.[1]

Imagine filling that centre every Sunday to its full capacity. Let's say each person tithes R5. (And, as we well know, no one pays R5 as a tithe; that's simply embarrassing. In many churches, people pay a tenth of their salary.)

That's what I am talking about when I say religion has become big business. Am I complaining? No. Just stating facts, and reflecting on them. I mean, drugs are big business; alcohol is big business; prostitution is big business. So why can't religion be big business?

The drug and alcohol businesses make their money by selling people the illusion of power and the ability to forget their troubles, albeit for a while. Prostitution offers the consumer carnal pleasures without the burden of having to commit to a relationship.

And what does religion sell people? It sells hope.

When I was growing up, we were sold the myth of a happy afterlife if we were meek and humble. For the meek shall inherit the earth, hallelujah. The message of the church (not all churches, of course; mainly the evangelical establishment) is that the more you pay the pastor, the more you can expect in return.

Where else will the pastor get the money to buy his Cadillac or his Buick? No, silly, it won't drop from the skies like manna. It shall come from your collective pocket, hallelujah!

That's why our people will take the last cents they have and give them to a man who owns a private jet and mansions all over the world. Because, through his poetry and oratory skills, he has told them to give and keep giving if they want to be as rich as him. He is selling them a dream.

Your pastor can make you do almost anything he says in order to have you prove to him that you are part of his loyal flock.

Pastor Lesego Daniel will tell you to eat grass to show your faith and loyalty – and you will grovel and do so in the hope that such an act of humility will allow a miracle to happen so that you can become rich. The Kenyan pastor, Reverend Njohi, has asked his female congregants to attend church services without panties or bras so 'God can enter their bodies easily'.[2] Many have succumbed to the holy man's saucy clarion call. Where will they stop?

Your pastor will make you part with 10 per cent of your salary because blessed is the hand that gives than that which receives. It is also written in the Holy Book that you shall give to Caesar what is Caesar's. You see, my friend, there is biblical justification for these things.

When I speak to people who believe in T.B. Joshua and other pastors like him, it seems that they do not view his ministry from a strictly spiritual perspective. Rather, they say 'he makes things happen' – suggesting that if they throw in their lot with him, sooner or later their ship will come into the harbour as well. He's a lotto dispenser of some sort. They say he was anointed by God.

Whether they are misguided or not is not for me to say. This here is just my contribution to getting people to see beyond the length of their noses, so to speak. Take it or leave, amen.

Walk the talk

Now that sushi (preferably eaten off a nearly naked human body) has lost its allure as the food of choice among Johannesburg's fashionable people, a new culinary curiosity has taken over the ranks: the humble chicken foot.

To be fair, my people have been eating chicken feet for as long as I can remember. It's just that in the Durban of my childhood, *ukuhamba kwayo* (literally, 'its walk'), as we used to call them, were mostly eaten by impecunious members of our community.

Just like eating chicken intestines, consuming chicken feet was something to be ashamed of, as it pointed to a lowly social status. Whenever my father slaughtered chickens – he had to slaughter two at a time as we were a huge family – he would give the feet to us children, not to eat, but to play 'house' with.

However, when we started eating them, having cooked them on our own fire in the yard, we realised how delicious they are. The 'big' people in the main house didn't know what they were missing.

Over the past few months, I have noticed chicken feet being served at several parties in Joburg. With my upturned nose, I used to refuse to partake of any dishes containing them. Even though I too had felt the effects of the recession, I refused to be humiliated like this.

In my mind, I believed that the hosts of these parties were looking down on me and my friends, giving us poor people's food, or food that I used to see as playthings when I was a child. Joburg people are strange when it comes to matters of the stomach; they serve every meal with atchar. Eggs, bacon and atchar in the morning. Braai meat and pap with atchar for lunch. Chicken stew, rice, veggies and atchar for dinner. If you are drinking and it's late at night, they will serve chips, wors and atchar as a snack.

I have been living in this city for sixteen years now, but I still can't get used to atchar. I have to admit that there are times when I do feel for some pickled fruit and vegetables with a meal; in the morning after a heavy night, for example. But I stopped eating this side dish when the *Sunday Times* broke a story some time ago that Sudan Red – that terrible toxic food dye – was being used in the preparation of atchar.[1]

The discovery gave me an excuse to politely inform my hosts that I could not have atchar for medical reasons. But another reason I stopped eating it was because somebody had told me that atchar left a long-lasting odour on your person, especially under the armpits.

But, ag, that's no way to write about food. Let's leave that atchar alone and focus on the delicacy of the moment: the chicken feet. Where I come from, chicken feet are things that ordinary people used to throw to the dogs. Turns out that over the years, especially in Joburg, chicken feet have been growing in popularity in mainstream culinary circles – so much so that food chains such as Pick n Pay have been selling chicken feet in bulk, nicely packaged and all.

I was astounded when I made this discovery, especially when I found out that chicken feet are stealing a march on other mainstream delicacies in restaurants, and are even being served at places such as Neh!, a popular spot frequented by fashionable types in Marlboro in northern Johannesburg. Patrons will tell you that the restaurant is situated in Alexandra, I suppose to give it street cred. But it's not in Alex. To make such a comparison is like saying that Alex is in Sandton.

Having visited Neh! and other fashionable eateries, I have discovered that the walkie-talkies are cooked in various mouth-watering ways. Some chefs simply dunk the feet in water and let them boil for hours until they are delicate and the meat (if that's what you can call it) falls off the bone. Others go to great lengths, lovingly preparing the chicken bits as they would a thick, rich stew. Ah, the gravy is to die for. Some cooks braai the chicken feet, and you will find a very popular corner in Alex proper which specialises in such braaied *maotwana*. On Monday evenings, you will spot sleek cars parked outside the eatery, the drivers munching on braaied *tincondzo*. But don't try this at home. You should call an expert if you want to braai chicken feet. When prepared by someone who knows what they are doing, the highly salted braai gristle will bring tears of joy to your eyes – especially if you are partaking of that amber nectar from the Scottish Highlands.

One downside to eating chicken feet is that you have to eat a lot of them in order to feel sated. Chicken feet being the latest big thing in South African fine dining is also problematic because you can't eat them off a naked person's body. They are definitely not sexy enough for that. Recently, however, a few fashionable guys in KwaZulu-Natal, not wanting to be outdone by their Joburg counterparts, attempted eating cow tripe off a woman's naked body. Their effort, while daring, was ill-fated, as you have to eat tripe while it is piping hot. Imagine a semi-naked beauty wincing in pain as you devour piping-hot tripe off her body. Not *ayoba*! Eating tripe is also a messy affair. It's fatty and very wet. And you don't want to eat it with a knife and fork as that would be considered sacrilege. You have to eat it the same way you would a bunny chow or curry and roti – with your hands.

So at present, and because you have to be careful how you eat them, chicken feet will remain snacks that will help you keep your feet firmly on the ground. In addition to the frustration of finding a place where you can bite into them, there's the challenge of preventing the gravy from dripping between your fingers, snaking along the corners of your mouth and staining your shirt. And sometimes you get a claw stuck between your front teeth. Now that's a sight.

The sushi types, resplendent in their expensive suits, will soon tire of chicken feet. Or at least that's what we commoners hope. I don't want to be mistaken for a BEE type as I tuck into my chicken feet at my local social club, which we have christened the Manqina (chicken feet) Social Club.

To sort of steal a leaf from Jimmy Manyi's book, let's reintroduce apartheid now – at least on culinary matters. Let Kenny Kunene, Khanyi Mbau and the rest of their class continue to eat their sushi from human platters. The rest of us will stick to our *manqina* and tripe. The class war has begun.

Sunday Times, 19 March 2011

Christmas with the Khumalos

At the beginning it was jolly good fun, but over the years entertaining members of my extended family – whether they come to my house in Johannesburg, or I visit them in my ancestral home in KwaZulu-Natal – has become something of a burden. The slaughter of the beast has lost its jovial sacredness. The allure has faded from the sharing of libations with uncles, aunts and cousins. As Christmas comes hurtling towards us, I can already sense the trouble approaching. That trouble is Uncle Ernest, my mother's brother.

There is something enigmatic about maternal uncles. Not only do they tend to be the black sheep in their families, but they are also social misfits. I don't know why. Maybe it's the way society views them: they are your blood, but not close enough to have the same surname as you. Your father doesn't like them either, because they invariably tried to stand between him and your mother in the days of courtship. Or they made him pay huge *ilobolo*.

So you generally side with your father in your dislike for your maternal uncles. Your paternal uncles – *obab'omncane* – are a different kind of adversary. They are always giving you dirty looks because they think your father is turning you into a spoilt brat. They expect him to be as hard on you as their father was on them.

'Khumalo boys are not supposed to do this, Khumalo boys are not supposed to speak like this … blah blah blah.' But they share your surname; they are Khumalos like you and you can't do anything about it.

Maternal uncles are almost dispensable, yet they stick to you like leeches, especially if you were born out of wedlock. My earliest recollection of my Uncle Ernest is that of an energetic man, flashily dressed and fast-talking, despite having a mouth devoid of front teeth.

As a boy of five I found it odd that such a big and good-looking man had no teeth. I thought toothlessness was the domain of new-born babies, or boys and girls just a year or two older than me, or ancient grandpas and grandmas who had tasted all the food in the world and no longer had any use for teeth. I'd wonder how he ate meat or what girls did when he smiled. 'He lost his teeth in jail,' my aunts would whisper behind my uncle's back. This was another enigma: jail. What place was so bad that it could deprive you of such important and basic ornaments as teeth?

Incidentally, Uncle Ernest was not the only male in our extended family who had just returned from prison. My oldest cousin, Mzala Zoo, had sat alongside my uncle in that seemingly dark and dank place. But while my uncle returned home with his strength dissipated, Mzala Zoo came back with a new body rippling with muscles.

This was in 1971 and my parents were not married yet, so, as is custom, I was living with my maternal grandparents in Chesterville, a township a short distance from Durban. Uncle Ernest and Mzala Zoo also stayed with us – when they were not in jail. During their stay, the two gentlemen would regale me and my cousins with tales about life in the big house. Mzala Zoo was always telling us how difficult it was and that we should study hard at school so we wouldn't end up being criminals. He was always exercising as well: shadow-boxing and running up and down the street – to keep fit and healthy, he would say. Then he would show us his latest boxing moves, which he said we should learn if we wanted to be respected on the streets. A hint of jealousy would usually flicker in Uncle Ernest's eyes every time we small boys joined Mzala Zoo under the huge avocado tree in the middle of the yard to learn how to shadow-box, screaming the fear of God into the heart of an imaginary adversary.

Uncle Ernest, though, would spit on the ground, his serpentine tongue protruding out of his gap-toothed mouth. He'd then brandish his huge knife and start slashing an invisible enemy with it, saying, 'People in the streets have no time for your boxing shit; they'll slash you like this with their knives while you are jumping about like a poor imitation of Muhammad Ali.'

I have to admit that his moves with the knife were impressive. Kids growing up in the ghetto fall easily under the guile of a man who carries a knife or gun. There is an aura of glamour and invincibility that surrounds such a man. Fighting it out with your bare hands is no child's play, as we would later learn when we attempted using the moves Mzala Zoo had tried to impart to us. We eventually opted for Uncle Ernie's knife-wielding tactics.

We kids also liked Uncle Ernest because he was talkative and funny, unlike the brooding Mzala Zoo. Serious and sullen people are dangerous because you never know when they are about to snap and give you a klap. But as I got older, I began to see Uncle Ernest for what he really was: a troublesome, insecure, attention-seeking brat who is ultimately useless without his knife. With that in mind, it came as no surprise to me that his teeth were punched out in prison.

A family gathering can never be complete without him causing a scene, either by calling my father a country bumpkin, or by complaining to everyone that his parents had set him up for failure by not sending him to high school – a blatant lie, as he dropped out of school of his own volition after all the caning my grandpa used to visit on his skinny ass.

I think that by now, you can begin to understand the kind of world my Uncle Ernie really lived in.

This is why the prospect of Christmas always brings to mind his name and all the things of which I know he is capable. I thought that with age, he would mellow. But not Uncle Ernest.

Not only has he not stopped living as a nomad with no fixed abode, but, whenever we have a family gathering, he continues to make himself the centre of attraction, and for all the wrong reasons. When someone threatens him with violence, he doesn't forget to mention that he is a baaad man. He has, if you don't recall, been to prison slews of times and is a Buthelezi by birth – a clan of warriors you shouldn't mess with. He also calls on his brother-in-law (my father), who is from the Khumalos, another baaaad clan of warriors. So don't mess with me, my boy. I'm covered.

However, if the person threatening him with violence hap-pens to be my father, Uncle Ernest just sulks, or pushes his tongue through the gap between his teeth, pointing an accusing finger at my father and shouting: '*Sbali* [brother-in-law], you shouldn't be so sure of yourself. Remember you never finished paying *ilobolo* for my sister. Your kids now have big beards yet you still haven't fin-ished paying *ilobolo*. A man like you should be the last one to show indiscretion towards his in-laws.'

It is unfortunate that the one person who could deal effectively with Uncle Ernest, my younger brother Cornelius, has passed on. Whenever Uncle Ernest started raving at people, Cornelius would always shout, 'Everybody reach for your raincoats! Uncle is going to wet your faces with his waterfall of saliva!'

This declaration – referring to the torrents of saliva that usually escape through the gap between Uncle Ernest's teeth when he starts shouting – would disarm Uncle Ernest, who would respond grump-ily and walk away, or succumb to a fit of laughter, in which event everybody really would need their raincoats.

So this Christmas I will have to deal with Uncle Ernest single-handedly. Whenever he commences with his antics, the older people turn their heads away and pretend he is not there. But to me he is a nuisance and a real shame and embarrassment, especially when my in-laws and friends are around. What is worse is that the bugger knows this, as well as the fact that I will do anything to shut him up. 'Okay, son of my sister,' he will lisp when he sees me clenching and unclenching my fists in anger, 'just give me a bottle of *ugologo obomvu* [brandy] and I will leave you in peace so you can sit down with your friends and speak all the English and the politics in the world.'

And if Uncle Ernest is insolence personified, then my paternal aunt Tee works on you like slow poison. By the time you finally recover from her spell, your pockets are dry. *'Awu, mntakabhuti* [Oh, my brother's child],' she says to me each time she sees me, 'how about some R200 for your old aunt so she can buy some pantyhose?'

I am left with so much guilt upon hearing this request that I find myself parting with the money before Tito Mboweni can say 'Tighten your belt'.

Later on, after she has disappeared from festivities for a while, she can be spotted dawdling down the streets, her legs buckling under her weight. *'Awu, mntakabhuti,'* she laments to me, 'these tsotsis are bad. They have taken all the money you gave to me. How about another R200?'

With this pronouncement, everybody in the yard will usually break out in laughter, because it is clear that she is full of beer. Nevertheless, out of pity, I give her more notes and she disappears, no doubt to look for another victim. Around New Year, she wears a morose face and sings a new tune: *'Awu, mntakabhuti,* my kids have to go back to school. Can't you arm me with a handful of rands so I can take care of their stationery?' This when everybody in the family knows that her kids have long dropped out of school. But even so, her charm still works.

My father's line during almost every family gathering is: 'Eish,

I wish my soccer team were still around. Look at Patrice Motsepe and Tokyo Sexwale. Look at their contribution to our soccer. If only I had a hotline to one of them. Perhaps they would help me resuscitate my team.'

You see, when I was a boy, my father used to own a soccer team that was relatively successful, ending up in the second division of the former National Professional Soccer League. In his heart of hearts, my father truly believes I have enough money to help him claw back to this enchanted past, and from the dustbins of history give him another chance to helm his own soccer team.

And yet, in spite of all the drama that will undoubtedly unfold at this year's gathering of the clan – the conflict, the loss of money and the dream-shattering – I still find myself salivating at the prospect of participating in it again. Reflecting on maternal uncles has had me wondering what my own sisters' children make of me. I will make a point of watching them closely this coming Christmas. Maybe they even have a nickname for me. Maybe they think I'm too stingy, or too aloof, or too in love with the waters of immortality.

To be a maternal uncle is definitely not child's play. I'm beginning to love Uncle Ernest all over again, and even look forward to his Christmas crap.

Sunday Times, **21 December 2005**

Acknowledgements

Thanks to all my Facebook friends without whom the profundities, proclivities, proclamations, proselytisations, provocations, protestations, problematisations, prognostications and other –ations and –ities in this book would not have happened. Thanks to my ramblings on Facebook, putting these scribblings into book form was easy, and yet also difficult. Easy because the pieces were long enough to hold their own within a book; difficult, because they sometimes run into each other, or contradict each other, battling for supremacy and visibility.

Truth be told, I would never have known I'd written a book had Ben Williams not raised this with me. 'I love your Facebook posts,' he told me when we bumped into each other at the Woolies in Rosebank in February 2016. 'I think they'll make a great book. Ever thought of that? Unlike the rest of us, when you tune into Facebook, you really make an effort. You *write*.' He even dropped in the word 'thought-provoking' at one point.

Another friend who echoed Ben was Vuyo Nxokwana, who said to me: 'With a bit of a massage here and there, your FB posts will make a highly readable book.' So thanks, guys, for waking me up. This is your book. Mark Zuckerberg? Thanks for nothing, thanks for nothing! This starving African brings so much traffic and respectability, so many pieces of beautiful writing and inoffensive interactions to Facebook, and yet you can't pay him a single red American cent for his efforts.

As for those who have read my other books: keep reading and keep provoking me with ideas. I am still on Facebook and I also tweet (look out for @FredKhumalo), although I am too long-winded for Twitter. I Instagram as well, regardless of the fact that it causes my teenage daughters to twist their faces and say, 'Yeouw, Dad, you're too old for Instagram,' whenever they catch me at it.

Notes

We've been having it!

1. 'Hugh Masekela Biography', *3rd Ear Music*, http://www.3rdearmusic .com/reissue/hughmasakela.html, last accessed 12 May 2016.

Alone among the Zulus – an Englishwoman's experience

1. Catherine Barter, *Alone Among the Zulus: The narrative of a journey through the Zulu country, South Africa*, ed. Patricia L. Merrett (Pietermaritzburg: Killie Campbell Africana Library Publications, 1995), p. 42.
2. See http://www.southafrica.info/about/people/language.htm#.VzQrn IR96Uk; http://mybroadband.co.za/news/broadcasting/160358- biggest-radio-stations-in-south-africa.html; http://www.marklives. com/2015/05/abc-analysis-q1-2015-the-biggest-circulating- newspapers-in-south-africa/.

#ZuptasMustFall

1. Editorial, 'Editorial: #Guptagate has a silver lining', *Mail & Guardian*, 18 March 2016.
2. Qaanitah Hunter and Sibongakonke Shoba, 'Zuma told me to help Guptas', *Sunday Times*, 20 March 2016.
3. Jan-Jan Joubert, 'Vytjie Mentor tearfully opens up about Guptas', *Sunday Times*, 19 May 2016.
4. Sapa, 'Waterkloof key point or not, Guptas, Zuma must be probed', *Mail & Guardian*, 20 May 2013.
5. Matuma Letsoalo, Jessica Bezuidenhout and Lisa Steyn, 'Gupta

family "edged me out of Eskom", says Tsotsi', *Mail & Guardian*, 18 March 2016.

6. 'Listen to EFF's new house track "Zupta Must Fall"', *Sunday World*, 20 March 2016.

7. Craig Dodds, 'Guptas can't bank on SA', *IOL*, 9 April 2016.

8. Matthew le Cordeur, 'Guptas and Duduzane Zuma resign from Oakbay', *fin24*, 8 April 2016.

Girl, you make that dress look good

1. Richard O. Boyer, 'The Hot Bach – I', *The New Yorker*, 24 June 1944.

Virgin brains

1. Mashoto Lekgau, 'Mshoza set for brand-new look', *Sowetan*, 8 January 2016.

What I meant was …

1. Steve Biko, *I Write What I Like: A selection of his writings* (South Africa: Picador Africa, 2004), p. 21.

How Google made me an intellectual eunuch

1. 'floccinaucinihilipilification', *Oxford Dictionaries*, http://www.oxford dictionaries.com/definition/english/floccinaucinihilipilification, last accessed 21 April 2016.

2. See 'The rise and impact of digital amnesia: Why we need to protect what we no longer remember', Kaspersky, https://blog.kaspersky.com /files/2015/06/005-Kaspersky-Digital-Amnesia-19.6.15.pdf, last accessed 29 April 2016.

3. Ibid., p. 8.

Me, me, me!

1. Joel Stein, 'Millennials: The Me Me Me Generation', *Time*, 20 May 2013.

2. Ibid.

Fan these fragrant winds of change
1. Michelle Obama, 'We still need to sacrifice', *Sowetan*, 23 June 2011.

No 'darkie' sarcasm in the class struggle
1. Statistics South Africa, 'Poverty trends in South Africa: An examination of absolute poverty between 2006 and 2011' (Pretoria: Statistics South Africa, 2014), pp. 12 and 26.

The rotund fence-jumper
1. News/Crime-Courts, 'Majority of SA thinks police are corrupt', *IOL*, 12 July 2013.

Amazing Grace!
1. Stephen Jakes, 'Grace does not love Mugabe – analyst', *Bulawayo24*, 2 November 2015.

Musical reflections
1. Hugh Masekela and D. Michael Cheers, *Still Grazing: The Musical Journey of Hugh Masekela* (New York City: Three Rivers Press, 2005).
2. David B. Coplan, *In Township Tonight! South Africa's Black City Music & Theatre* (Johannesburg: Jacana Media, 2008), p. 231.
3. 'Miriam Makeba's historic speech remembered', PRI's The World, 11 November 2008, http://www.pri.org/stories/2008-11-10/miriam-makebas-historic-speech-remembered, last accessed 30 May 2016.

The fine and terrible line that apartheid collaborators walked
1. Jacob Dlamini, *Askari: A Story of Collaboration and Betrayal in the Anti-Apartheid Struggle* (Johannesburg: Jacana Media, 2014).
2. Ibid.

What is a national key point?
1. The list of national key points has since been revised. A new list was published on 16 January 2015 at http://www.r2k.org.za/wp-content/uploads/List-of-National-Key-Points.pdf.

Cure this man of his gout, or else …

1. Alistair Bunkall, 'North Korea: Kim Jong-un official speaks', *Sky News*, 30 January 2014.

For the meek shall inherit the earth, amen

1. Mfonobong Nsehe, 'The Five Richest Pastors in Nigeria', Forbes, 7 June 2011.
2. Radhika Sanghani, '"Bra and knickers? Sorry, not in my church"', *The Telegraph*, 4 March 2014.

Walk the talk

1. Megan Power and Jocelyn Maker, 'From the archive: Tainted products could put you at risk of cancer', *Times Live*, 16 October 2014.

Coming soon from Fred Khumalo

Death Drill, a historical novel inspired by the tragic sinking of the *SS Mendi*, a ship carrying over 800 black soldiers from South Africa to fight in World War I.